SILENT SCREAMS

PART ONE

BASED ON REAL LIFE STORIES

MATTHEW MARIN

US NAVY VETERAN AND POLICE OFFICER

ISBN-13: 978-1-970079-58-6

Published by Opportune Independent Publishing Company

For permission requests, write to the publisher, addressed "Attention: Permissions Coordinator" to the address below.

Email: Info@opportunepublishing.com

Address: 113 N. Live Oak Street
Houston, TX 77003

Edited by my beautiful sister Morgan Bass

Contact her for editing at morgankbass@gmail.com

Table of Contents

Chapter 11:

Chapter 12:

Chapter 13:

BATTLE BUD

P O D C A S T

The Battle Bud podcast will be going over trauma stories and interviewing trauma victims, understanding their story and learning their coping skills.

BATTLE BUD
Y O U ' R E N E V E R A L O N E

For donations or bookings in support of veterans and officers; look us up at Birdwellfoundation.org. Donations will go towards providing Peer Support resources to veterans and first responders who are suffering from PTSD.

Introduction

This book provides an inside look into the life of a police officer, based on actual experiences on the job. This book is meant to help families and friends of officers understand what their loved ones experience as they protect our communities and how that affects their everyday lives. More importantly, this book is for people who want to better understand PTSD and what one can expect both mentally and physically as a result. Not everyone experiences the same symptoms, but I hope by sharing my personal story it will help others to know that they are not alone.

Please note that I am not a licensed psychologist or medical professional, but am sharing what I have learned about PTSD from my personal experiences and others I have interviewed. Any statistics that I share will be accompanied with sources.

Due to the demanding nature of the job, police officers often bring their work home with them, whether they want to or not. As a police officer with 13 years of experience, I know firsthand that bringing the job home can manifest itself in various ways and in turn affect relationships with both family and friends.

I received a football scholarship right out of high school, but joined the U.S. Navy after my first year of college. In the military, I completed 4.5 nine-month tours overseas – on both the USS John F. Kennedy which is an aircraft carrier, and on the USS Boxer (LHD-4), an amphibious ship. My time in the military had its own toll on my state of mind but those effects became painfully clear by the time I garnered some years as a Police Officer. Oddly enough, I witnessed damaging scenes as an officer far more than I ever experienced during my time in the military.

I would later experience episodes where I either tried to force myself to cope by engaging in life's indulgences or by burying it all deep down with the hope it would go away – it was not working. I was at a point where I needed to get therapy and heal from the accumulated impact Post Traumatic Stress Disorder (PTSD) was having on my everyday life. PTSD is a disease of the mind which plagues more veterans and active servicemen than we might imagine. Unfortunately, many people do not prioritize getting the help and healing that they need, even as the weight of our career continues to pile up. It was not until I sought out the necessary help and committed to the journey of processing my trauma that I have learned to live and not just survive. Committing to making it work and inviting in my friends and family helped me to work through the pain and burden of PTSD has made all the difference. While I am lucky to still be intact after living with the silent screams that have ravaged my mind for so long, many others are not so lucky.

My experience during the past 13 years has allowed me to see the worst and the best in people. It has also taken me through the vast highs and lows of life. This is why I love my job and cannot imagine myself doing anything else in life. Hopefully, the short stories that follow will help you understand what we go through on a daily basis. It is my hope that this book provides a practical guide to understanding how to care for our loved ones that balance protecting our cities and risking their lives and mental health every day.

"No one will be the same. The people who have PTSD, both those who were hit by bullets and those who were in that area when it happened. It is a very, very debilitating condition and they are suffering on a daily basis, and families have been broken apart."

~Neil Sher, Lead Attorney for the Prosecution of Nazi criminals

Chapter 1:
The Genesis of My Life in The Forces

A lot of times, special events in the life of kids influence the career they are devoted to pursuing. The desire to pursue such a career is even stronger when one of the parents is a professional in that field. I recall vividly that an event where my dad played center-stage when I was little influenced my decision to be in the Forces later in life.

Watching a Hero

My father is a hard ass who has been through a ton of trauma in his life. He has experienced being homeless and sleeping under bridges at a young age, drowning and then being revived while he was in the Marine Corps, and when he was in the police force, he once rammed a car full of criminals to save the lives of other officers who were pinned down. (This particular incident left my old man with a totaled patrol car, minor injuries, and a mouth full of beautiful new veneers). When I was 10 years old, we lived in an apartment complex in

My old man in his prime

South Houston. I remember hearing gunshots almost nightly and people screaming for help outside my apartment window. For the most part, I do not have many detailed memories of my childhood, but there is one that I remember like it was yesterday. I was with my dad, and we were home watching Scarface, a cinematic classic. This kind of movie is not what many parents would normally deem appropriate for a 10 year old to be watching, but my old man was always saying that I would see it anyways when I grew up. When my loving mother would confront him on issues like letting a child watch murder and drug use, he just shrugged her off by saying " he's a boy!" knowing she would just drop it. This particular evening, we started to hear screaming outside near our apartment door. We really didn't think much of it at first because where we lived, it was common to hear screaming all hours of the day and night. However, this time it was closer than usual.

Soon after the screams, we heard pounding on our front door. Someone was yelling and screaming for help. I watched my father jump up and open the door, and standing there was a young woman yelling that her apartment was on fire and that her baby was trapped inside. My dad, who was wearing his white undershirt and black Daisy Duke Shorts, ran to the apartment directly across from ours. It was on the second floor across the sidewalk. I could actually see from my doorstep the apartment that was on fire and the black smoke pouring from the edges of the door. My dad made his way down our stairs across the sidewalk and back up the stairs to her front door where he took off his shirt, wrapped it around his fists and broke the glass to the front window which was located right next to the front door of the burning apartment.

After breaking the window, smoke started pouring out, allowing air to get inside. My dad had to kick the door down to get into the apartment because the woman accidentally locked her door when she ran out. Without hesitation, my dad ran into the burning apartment and came out quickly, back and forth a number of times, to catch his breath and every time he came out his cough got louder and louder until finally he coughed up black mucus and saliva from inhaling the smoke.

My old man just before retirement

By this time, everyone was gathered around outside the apartments. Many people were trying to get him to stop and give up because the apartment was engulfed in flames, but my father just told them to hold on. He wanted to go in one more time, and ran back into the apartment. As I watched from our balcony with my hands gripped onto the railing, I remember wondering if I would see him alive again. He was inside for what felt like forever to the point where everyone started worrying and screaming for somebody to go in after him to drag him out. I remember seeing a man getting ready to go in after my father when at the very last second my Dad came crawling out of the apartment with the baby in his hands.

Standing off to the side, I immediately saw the reaction of the people who had gathered and were worried about him and the baby inside the burning apartment. I also saw how grateful everyone was that he actually had the guts to take action and go into the fire. Being as young as I was and seeing what my dad did is something that I find hard to describe. Following this incident, my father received praise from the police department, earned a lifesaving award, and also had an article written about him saving the child. My father was a hero in my eyes and at a very young age, his actions helped me form a pretty clear decision on what I wanted to do in life.

After this, I remember having very vivid dreams about this incident repeatedly throughout my childhood and into adulthood. I sometimes dreamed of him never coming back out from the burning apartment and I would wake up crying or sweating with my heart pounding so hard it felt like it could burst out of my chest. As a result, I often feared that I would never see my father again when he left for work as I now understood that his job would involve him making life-changing decisions like the one I witnessed firsthand. Additionally, I developed a fear of fire and found myself constantly striving for my father's approval. While I was in awe of my Dad's heroism that was also an experience that I can now identify as a traumatic event in my childhood that truly affected me. It is vital that parents learn how to recognize signs of trauma in children so that they can get the help they need, learn from their experience, and carry on with being a child.

Dad's Meritorious Service Award

When I went to college on a football scholarship, it did not take long for me to become bored and search for something more. After the attacks on 9/11 I felt that what I was looking for could be found in the military and ended up enlisting in the US Navy as soon as I could.

My time in the military definitely shaped how I approached policing and how I react in certain situations, for better or for worse. Looking back to my days in Navy training, I can honestly say that Boot Camp was an eye opener. Young men from all over the United States are placed together in a "ship" also known as our boot camp unit. Here I had experienced how others lived and acted in close quarters. Teamwork was not foreign to me because I participated in organized sports since I was very young, but boot camp helped me to see challenging situations as approachable and bolstered my work ethic.

One incident in the Navy that has continued to stay with me was an accident between our ship and a fishing vessel. On July 22, 2004, I was manned up on the USS John F. Kennedy aircraft carrier. I was on the bow of the ship in the catwalk, near the flight deck while we were recovering aircrafts. We were out in the Persian Gulf close to Bahrain. It was very foggy out, and I could not really see very far in front of the ship's bow- only maybe 10 to 15 yards out from the side of the ship. I spotted a wooden fishing boat just before we collided into it. I immediately dropped to the metal grated "catwalk" which allows you to see through to the water. I saw some men screaming and waving at us, and so I braced myself for impact and a possible explosion by grabbing the grating and shutting my eyes, not knowing if I would be able to open them again. We felt a hard jerk of the ship and heard a loud bang, which was the breaking of the wood crashing into the water. I was scared as hell that it was a bomb since just four years prior, the USS Cole was bombed by fishing boats carrying explosives. As I opened my eyes back up to see the damage I couldn't breathe right for a few seconds, it literally took my breath away. I will never forget seeing the aftermath of the bodies of the thirteen fishermen that died that day and the broken wood slowly sinking to the bottom of the Persian Ocean.

In my line of work as a police officer, I have seen plenty of dead bodies. But since I left the military, I have had continuous flashbacks of bodies floating and pieces of the boat under me in the water. For the most part it happens at night, but in my job when I encounter a scene where there is a dead body in the water or a floater I have learned to focus on my task at hand and redirect my thoughts., when I hear men yelling in my dreams, I wake up in cold sweats to the visions of the JFK blowing up and me being blown off the flight deck, every dream is different but most all versions includes the ship blowing up. To this day, I am fearful of fishing and avoid being near big bodies of water whenever possible.

Early Warning Signs

Now that I look back on it, it seems quite weird. I actually had a few early warning signs that my career as a police officer would be highly stressful and action packed. One of those signs came on my first day off the field training program. I was finally a police officer and done with all of my training so I was finally able to ride by myself. I was on the dayshift early side unit while waiting on my cadet class to pick where everyone wanted to work which would take a few weeks.

I arrived at roll call a little early to get all my equipment and relax a little before the other officers showed up for work. As I was sitting there by myself, nervous about my first day, a sergeant who used to be my dad's old partner years ago came out from his office in a hurry, yelling "Marin lets go! Get in the car!"

I grabbed my radio and took off behind him thinking, "Damn! I'm not even supposed to be here yet! "As I jumped into the passenger side of the patrol car. The sergeant and an administrative officer with civilian clothes dove into the backseat as we were backing out of the driveway. I did not know what was going on until my sergeant turned on the radio in the patrol car.

I quickly learned that a chase was going on and that it started with an undercover officer sitting up on the house of a suspect who had two separate warrants for aggravated sexual assault of a child. Somehow, he got wind of the cops outside of his home and he slid out the back door with his father, jumped into his dad's small red pickup truck, and took off toward downtown Houston, disregarding lights and sirens from a patrol unit that was on standby with the undercover officer.

As we made our way to the intersection that he was approaching, we were able to pull up directly behind the first patrol car and get into the chase. The suspect was traveling at a speed of approximately 60 miles an hour through residential areas. He finally lost control and crashed into a tree after an officer threw out spikes that perfectly blew out the front driver's side tire. The suspect, who was a young Hispanic male, jumped out of his vehicle with a gun and pointed it toward us while we were sliding to a stop. As we exited the patrol car, I heard a lot of gunshots from officers and saw the suspect get shot in the chest. He turned and ran down the street, looking back periodically pointing the gun at officers running after him.

Every time he turned and pointed the gun at the officers, you could see his shirt jerking in different directions from the bullets from the officers' guns. Because I was running behind officers that were shooting, I was unable to take a clean shot at him. After being shot numerous times, the suspect then somehow jumped onto someone's porch and tried to kick in the door. After the second kick, another officer went around the house to get a better look at him and shot him as he was turning around with his gun pointing at the officer. After being shot on the porch, the suspect then stumbled onto the front yard and eventually fell near the sidewalk, face up. When I got to him an officer took the gun away from him as he was laying there, breathing heavily and almost lifeless. His body was riddled with bullet holes and blood poured out of every wound, leaving him unable to speak. The sergeant told me to find something to slow the blood loss - so I went door-to-door asking neighbors if they had anything to stop the bleeding. I finally got some saran wrap at the third house and we wrapped his upper body tightly with it and temporarily stopped the bleeding until the ambulance arrived and took him away. Apparently, the suspect had been shot 13 times. Fortunately for him, after months of multiple surgeries and rehab, he was able to walk and talk normally again.

Three days after witnessing my first shooting, I soon had another crazy episode at work. When I got to the station that morning, I was paired up with another older officer who happened to have worked on patrol with my dad when they were rookies. He was a nice guy who knew his job inside and out - especially how to handle situations quickly. I had heard my father and some other officers speak very highly of him as an officer.

As soon as we loaded up the patrol car, the radio blasted a call regarding "a suspicious person, black male, wearing a tan jacket, harassing people." On our way there, my partner was messing with me about how young I was and about how my father was a crazy man who wouldn't accept anything mediocre from anybody. This was a fact that I have witnessed many times, he could be an asshole at times. However, I still loved those stories when others would talk about the good my dad did as a cop. It motivated me to strive to be as good of an officer as he was.

When we arrived at the address, we found a Hispanic male wearing a black hoodie, pacing back and forth in the street in front of his house. We parked the patrol car in a position where we could get out safely if we needed to. We approached the man and asked how he was doing, not knowing for sure if this was our guy. Before I got the words out of my mouth, he started yelling at us.

"Leave me alone! Why are y'all motherfuckers fucking

with me all the time?"

I turned to my partner and muttered under my breath, "Yup, this has to be our guy."

The suspect was definitely not a black male as was radioed earlier. At times, call takers get these details confused when speaking to people who are scared and in turn hard to understand. The suspect was also clearly under the influence of narcotics. His pinpoint pupils were our first clue, and his aggression toward us confirmed this assessment.

When I approached him, he backed away from us and ran inside a house. Within seconds, he ran back outside, charging toward us with his shirt off and fists balled up, ready to fight.

He was screaming, "Come on motherfuckers! Y'all want some!?"

I yelled "Stop!" He wasn't slowing down. I pulled my Taser out of its holster and waited for him to get within seven feet from me. I shot him in his chest, hitting the mark. The suspect immediately fell to the ground; screaming and yelling in pain. I ordered him to lie on his stomach, face down, but he continued to yell.

"Fuck you! Fuck...fuck!"

Then he surprised us. He started log-rolling away from us, breaking the wires connected to the Taser. In doing so, he was able to set himself free. As he struggled to get up, his mother came out of nowhere and grabbed my arm, pleading for me to stop. She kept yelling that her son was "not trying to hurt anybody."

The situation was escalating quickly. The son grabbed his mother by her hair knocking her to the floor and started dragging her toward the front of the porch stairs. Then he grabbed her and they both scrambled into the house. My partner quickly followed them inside with his duty weapon drawn. In the midst of all the confusion, I had been trying to reload my single shot Taser; and making my way to the door when I heard my partner yell, "Knife!"

As soon as I stepped inside, the suspect ran from a back bedroom, charging us with two huge knives held over his head. His mother stood in front of my partner's gun, which was pointed in the direction of the suspect making it impossible to fire a shot without endangering the lady trying to protect her son from harm's way. My partner stepped aside while shielding the mother from her son and yelled to me "I don't have a shot!"

As I attempted to use my Taser again, only one of the two darts from the Taser deployed, producing only a loud noise from the initial release of the functional dart deploying. Luckily for us, remembering the pain from the first blast, the suspect anticipated the second bolt, so he dropped one of his knives, fell to the ground, and log-rolled underneath a huge oak bed in the kitchen area, two feet away from where he fell.

The suspect still had one knife, so I quickly called for a backup unit and a supervisor to check on us. Both of us were commanding the suspect to get rid of the knife and to come out from under the bed. He refused our order, all the while cursing at us from underneath the bed.

When the back-up units arrived, we all tried dragging the suspect out by his feet, but he didn't budge because he wrapped his legs steadfastly around the bed's leg. A sergeant soon got fed up with the suspect's behavior and directed us to "drive stun" him, which is a tactic that deploys the Taser without the darts. It requires the Taser to be placed directly on the suspect's skin while pulling the trigger, giving them direct contact with the weapon. As I tasered the man on his inner right thigh, he bellowed in pain. He then straightened out both legs as if he just got struck by lightning, giving us just enough time for the other officers to drag him out from under the bed and onto the porch. He was still kicking and screaming, trying to get away from the four of us.

Each of us then grabbed an arm or a leg, counted to three, hoisted up the suspect, walked to the patrol car, and placed him in the backseat. To avoid further injury, we made sure to secure the suspect in the back seat of the patrol car to where he could not be a threat to himself or others. While all of this is going on, the suspect was still cursing and trying to break free from us.

After we dealt with this unruly guy, we returned to deal with his mother, who by now was completely distraught. We explained to her that she should never interfere with a police investigation because she might cause harm to herself or someone else. She agreed that she would "never do that again" and understood why it could be dangerous.

Since no one was hurt and all of the officers were okay, we used our discretion and did not arrest the mother for interfering. We knew that she could have caused injuries or death if I was not entering the house at that exact moment, but in this case, she literally saved her child's life as he charged my partner. Luckily, this call ended with no one getting hurt or killed.

To this day, I have dreams of this call and every different

scenario there could have been. I often wake up in the middle of the night sweating and breathing heavily after dreaming that either my partner or I ended up getting stabbed by the suspect.

Chapter 2:
Dealing with Drunk Drivers, Drug Abusers, and Domestic Altercations

Fighting a Drunk

When dealing with intoxicated people driving, I believe it is vital to not underestimate what they can do at any point in time. Their actions can be similar to that of someone who is mentally ill, and even go to the extreme of not caring if others are harmed in situations that do not even require self-defense. I could never have imagined that an intoxicated man could want to kill me without provocation – until it happened.

In the beginning of 2009, I was still a rookie on the DWI Task Force making at least three DWI arrests a night. During my first month in that unit, I started getting comfortable running the entire traffic stop field sobriety testing videos and reports needed for each arrest that was made. One night during my second month with the unit, I spotted an old 1980s model Ford Pickup truck swerving in and out of lanes on the Gulf Freeway heading southbound.

When I got a safe distance behind him, I pressed record

on my dash camera to capture my probable cause of the traffic stop I was about to make. After about 15 seconds of videotaping him bouncing in and out of his lane, I turned on my emergency lights and he started making his way to the far-right lane so he could get off the freeway. As he was exiting the freeway, I notified the dispatcher of my location, along with the license plate number and description of the vehicle. The man pulled onto a side road where the street was narrow and had ditches on either side. After the license plate check came back clear and there were no warrants, I slowly approached the vehicle on the driver side door, walking along the edge of a small ditch that was dried up and littered with trash.

When I approached the driver, he appeared to be very calm, but I could tell that he was intoxicated by his bloodshot eyes and slurred speech. While he was looking for his driver's license in his wallet, I could see that this was a very large man wearing workout shorts and a dirty white T-shirt which was stained with sweat. As I quickly scanned the inside of his truck, amid the filth, I saw a half empty bottle of whiskey lying on the passenger seat. When the driver handed his license to me, I noticed it was expired which gave me another reason to pull him out of the vehicle. I then asked him to please step out of the vehicle. I told him to be careful and watch his step because of the ditch he was parked against. After getting him to the back of his truck near his tailgate, we were standing in between my patrol vehicle and his pick-up truck with about a five-yard distance between the two vehicles. As I started speaking to him, I double checked to make sure my audio was on and my video was still recording by the little red dot of light on my front windshield. After verifying that everything was being recorded, I went ahead and started asking him questions about his night. I asked him where he was coming from and he answered me by saying "That's none of your damn business". When I asked how many drinks he had, he said "I had some whiskey a few hours ago, I don't know how much though maybe a few sips". I asked him when the last time he ate was, and he admitted he ate some BBQ at noon- it was 3am at that point.

When I asked him if he knew why I pulled him over, he responded saying "I have no idea- to harass me? I wanna go home now". I then replied "I pulled you over because you could not stay in your one lane and you were swerving on the freeway". After explaining why I pulled him over, he apologized and said "I just wanted to go home". I asked "If you do some tests for me and pass them you can go home". He agreed and then thanked me for giving him the opportunity to prove that he was not intoxicated.

As I was explaining to him how to do the walking turn test, he seemed to be watching me closely while asking questions along the way. After answering all of his questions, he started performing the test, and failed miserably. After he was finished, I gave him the opportunity to do another test and he agreed. As I was explaining the one leg stand test to him, I showed him how to perform the test by raising my right foot, looking down, and counting to ten. In those short moments, my eyes were totally off of him and on my raised foot, which led to me being totally unaware of what was about to transpire.

Because we were within 3 feet from each other, I did not have time to react when he lunged toward me, punching me on the left side of my face. As he punched me, I instinctively grabbed his shirt and brought him down with me as I fell back into the ditch. After rolling a few times, he ended up on top of me with my back on the ground, on top of the trash at the bottom of the ditch. I immediately started punching upwards towards his face, some missing and some hitting their mark, while also dodging the punches coming down toward me. As I was fighting him off of me, I felt him reach for my gun with his left hand and then use his other arm to put all his weight down on my other hand. I grabbed him and tried to roll on my side, pivoting my hips to where it would be hard for him to pull my gun out of my holster on my right hip. At the same time, I tried to get help from my radio, which at this point was wrapped around my neck.

This went on for a few more seconds with the both of us punching each other and wrestling for my gun. I could feel myself losing strength from each punch he was delivering to me. The weight of him was beginning to overpower me, and in one quick move, I was able to grab my gun and roll on my side to keep him from pulling it out. As I did so, I heard screeching tires and saw another officer running down the ditch, and before I knew it, the guy was pulled off of me and two officers had him on the ground with his hands behind his back after tasering him to release his hold on me.

I was out of breath and could feel my face cut up and blood dripping from my wounds. I slowly got up, dusted myself off, tried to fix my torn shirt, and unwrapped my radio that was around my neck. The officers stood the man up, walked him to a patrol car, and placed him in the backseat where he was later transported to the jail and booked for assaulting a police officer.

After taking down all the information about the suspect and the officers that showed up to help me, I requested an ambulance to clean up the wounds on my face. Afterward, I went back to my station and wrote my report for the incident and filed charges on the man. I can honestly say if it wasn't for those two officers who showed up just in time, I may not have been able to fight him off from taking my gun and could have lost my life as a result. I will occasionally have dreams at night about me not being able to move and being helplessly pinned under this man that was much larger than me as he gains control of my weapon. I wake up sweating and breathing heavily as I dream of him shooting me with my own weapon and leaving me to die alone in that ditch. That was a hard lesson learned that night: never take your eyes off of the suspect.

Triggered by Jealousy

The East end of Houston is known to be a predominantly Hispanic community with a lot of apartment complexes and low-income housing located around the ship channel. Many residents in this area refer to it as the "barrio". A lot of domestic violence occurs in this area, and most of it ends up unreported because of the culture there. Officers take these calls very seriously when we get them. Oftentimes, they are very dangerous situations which an officer doesn't want to find themselves in.

The call for help came from a woman living in an old apartment complex, saying that her ex-boyfriend was outside trying to kick in the door and threatening her and her kids who were inside the apartment. It turns out the man who was kicking the door was her ex-boyfriend who found out the woman was dating another man.

Eyewitnesses also stated that he had a metal pipe in his hand and had been drinking. Two other officers and I were very close to the scene finishing up another call, so we swung by.

When we arrived at the apartment complex, we noticed that it was not gated and there were no lights outside any of the apartments. When we got to the woman's apartment, no one was outside, but when the young mother of four small children opened the door, the look in her eyes was of fear and she could not stop crying. We took down all the information to make a report and told her to call if it happens again.

Before I walked out, I glanced at the faces of the kids who were so scared that one of them urinated on herself. I felt bad that we didn't catch the guy. We all worried the bad guy would come back to the apartment later, so we split up and searched the surrounding neighborhoods for him with a description given to us by the young woman. After about five minutes of driving around, the dispatcher called us to the same apartment because he came back and was breaking down the door by kicking it in. We immediately headed that way. She told us he said he was waiting for the police to leave and yelled, "I won't stop until you're dead!" The scared kids locked themselves in the bathroom this time.

I inspected the door for damages and saw the wooden frame was giving in and breaking, and a perfect footprint was on the outside of the door from the man bashing it in. My sergeant wanted us to go looking for him, believing that the guy was close by. The woman and her kids started pleading with us to stay with them. I told my sergeant that I thought it would be a good idea if I stayed with the family to see if he came back and if he does, I would bump them over the radio to close in on him. After inspecting the damage he did to the door and realizing the seriousness of the situation, the sergeant agreed with the plan. He told me to be careful as they walked out of the apartment and back to his patrol car. He got on the air and let me know that they pulled around the block to wait for my command. I sat on a broken chair at their kitchen table while waiting for the intruder to come by once more, going over different scenarios in my head of what could happen.

I told the kids to go to their room and lock the door and to not open it unless they heard my voice or their mother's voice telling them to do so. They agreed and quickly ran to the room locking the door, crying all the way. The mother was thanking me for staying with them and was apologizing for everything that was happening. I told her it was not her fault and that she should try to relax for the sake of the kids.

Three minutes went by in complete silence and then I felt the pounding vibrations of someone running up the steps of the apartment complex right outside connected to the balcony.

The man then yelled, "I know you keep calling the police, Bitch! That ain't stopping me!"

I jumped up, got my taser out, and notified the other officers that he was back via my radio. He started kicking the door hard, and then I motioned for the mother to move into the small kitchen. The man gave one last kick that broke the door open, slamming it against a small glass coffee table on the other side, causing it to flip over and break. His eyes and mine met and his rage quickly turned into fear. He raised the metal pipe that he had in his hand, and I quickly tasered him hitting his stomach and chest area. He immediately fell to the ground and by that time, my brothers were running up the stairs to help me place him under arrest. As we took him down the steps he yelled at his ex-girlfriend, "I'm going to kill you when I get out, Bitch!"

I assured the woman that on top of his charges, he got another charge for threatening her. The woman was so relieved we caught him and was very thankful. We got the children out of the room, but I could tell by the looks on their faces that they were still very, very scared. When their mother explained to them that the police caught the man and he will not be back to bother them anymore, they all gave a shy smile, then ran up to hug each of us, with tears rolling down their faces.

Calls like this give us officers some self-gratification and a mix of renewed belief in the system, knowing that the family is safe because of the actions we took to ensure their safety. But such scenarios often paralyze us too as we know that we can't always be quick enough to curtail every situation innocent citizens find themselves in. There will be times we will make the wrong call and/or we can't enforce the law in some instances because we have been outsmarted.

Officers who really care about what they do and the safety of others will go the extra mile to help people in need. There were so many ways that this situation could have turned out. In this case, we had the best possible outcome. Other times, it may go in the wrong direction. This is one of the things that constantly worries us and keeps us awake at night.

Driving Under Influence

When we were done with the domestic violence case, I wrote my report specifically elaborating on the reason I made the decision to wait until the door was kicked in despite posing potential danger to the terrified woman and her children. While I was finishing the report at the station, a call came from dispatch saying there was a major accident in the avenues involving two vehicles.

As I made it to the listed address, I noticed people standing outside of their homes pointing in the same direction. I didn't know what they were saying, but as I made my way over to the small Nissan that was turned over, I noticed a young man hanging upside down by his seatbelt with his face all cut up from the windshield falling on him. I pulled my knife from my pocket and started cutting into the seatbelt. As I was cutting I noticed blood pouring from the man's face; from the deep cuts made by the shards of glass under his chin. I warned him that he was going to fall and to protect his face as I finished cutting the seat belt to set him free.

The man had a short fall to the ground, I drug him out by placing my arms under his armpits, pulled him out from underneath the vehicle, and then laid him on the grass. The ambulance pulled up and medics rushed over to him to attend to his wounds. All of a sudden I heard my name being called out behind me, and when I turned around I noticed my Tia and her husband standing there. I forgot they lived in this neighborhood.

They told me they saw what happened, who did it, what car they were driving, and then tried their best to describe the man and his vehicle to me. I gave the description over the air and had officers on the lookout for the vehicle, noting that it may have a lot of damage on the front of it. Luckily, an officer spotted the vehicle soon after I gave the description over the air in front of a home that was not far from the accident. The other officers and I met at the house where the vehicle was parked. As we walked near the vehicle that fit the description I felt the hood and it was still warm, indicating it was just parked.

Two officers went to the back of the house in case he would try to run out the back door. When I knocked on the front door, a lady in her forties opened it and I could immediately see how nervous she was because her face was turning red and her breathing was getting very heavy. I asked her where the man was who drove that vehicle, as I pointed toward the red car. She claimed to not know anything about the vehicle at all. Another officer ran the plates of the vehicle in his patrol car and notified me over the radio that it was registered to this address, her face dropped knowing there was nothing else she could say and pointed to the back of the house where the man was hiding. As soon as we walked inside he jumped up from behind a couch in the living room and ran into the hallway.

He ran into a room and tried to shut the door on us, but we were able to power our way in and wrestle him to the ground. I immediately smelled alcohol on him, as we were placing him under arrest. Slurring his words, he repeatedly yelled, "Who ratted me out!?"

After placing him in the back seat and speaking to him,

he claimed that he didn't even know he hit another vehicle. I told him the car he hit flipped over in a ditch and injured the man driving, and that he was transported to the hospital for stitches. He started crying and apologizing and blaming everyone other than himself for the accident. Drunken people can be so unpredictable.

He Threw the Baby

On a busy night, we got a call near our station on the east end of Houston that a fight just broke out at a party going on at an apartment complex.

As I pulled up into the driveway, I could clearly see that the party was on the second floor because there were a number of people yelling and screaming over blaring music. I also had three other cop cars show up with me because of the big crowd at the scene. As we got out of our vehicles, we saw a man on the balcony of where the party was, holding an infant over his head yelling, "I'm gonna do it!"

Without hesitation, he threw the infant as far as he could over the balcony. It seemed like all of the officers yelled at the same time to stop, as the baby was in the air falling to the ground. We all rushed to the infant as soon as he hit the ground. We knew we needed to get him to the hospital immediately. When we got to the baby, he was not crying, he was not breathing.

A few officers stayed with him until the ambulance arrived while I, along with four other officers, rushed up to the apartment to apprehend the suspect who threw the baby off the balcony. As we approached the apartment, we had to push through many of the people who were all standing in the stairwells and in the hallways. When we got into the apartment, everyone pointed to the bedroom yelling, "He went in there!"

We rushed to the bedroom, not knowing if there were any weapons. We broke through the door that was locked and found our suspect in the corner of the room with a baseball bat yelling at us, "One of y'all is getting busted over the fucking head!"

He quickly jumped on top of the bed and was met by bolts of electricity from the Taser of a fast acting officer with us, making the suspect fall off the bed and drop to the floor. As soon as he went down, we jumped on top of him, took the baseball bat away from him, put his arms behind his back, and placed handcuffs on him. While I escorted him down the stairs and into the patrol car, the other officers got witnesses to give them statements about the baby getting thrown off the balcony. Then, they also cleared the apartment and shut down the party.

After interviewing the owner of the apartment, a young 20-year-old woman, we learned that he thought she was cheating on him and grabbed the baby and ran to the balcony. The officers went to the hospital to check up on the baby while another officer and I took the suspect to jail to file charges against him.

Miraculously, the baby was okay and no one got hurt. I often see this baby in my dreams falling, and every time I wake up scared and yelling unknown pleas right before the baby hits anything. It's weird what the brain keeps in your memory bank to torment you with later.

It was all a Blur

Starting the night shift by roaming the streets of South Houston is never a good way to avoid a busy night. Sometimes you pray not to encounter alarming situations at night like the instance where that poor baby was thrown over the balcony by a deranged man. These situations affect officers and everyone that is a witness to them as well. Everyone that is involved needs to address it with a professional to help understand the impact it has on you.

One night I was driving through the east end of Houston - a part of the city that is known for gang activity and burglaries. I didn't hear or see anything out of order, which surprised me a little, considering the neighborhood I was in and the experiences I have had in the past in this area.

As I pulled up to the red light, there was a small tan sedan at the other side of the intersection facing me. I could clearly see the driver punching himself in the face and slamming his head into the steering wheel while screaming at the top of his lungs. I could hear him loud and clear because both of our windows were down. Concerned, I went through the intersection and made a U-turn, parking directly behind the man's vehicle without him even acknowledging me. I ran his license plate on our computer and learned that the car was listed as stolen, so I grabbed the radio and notified dispatch of our location, and the situation I was in. I also asked for another unit to start heading my way, just in case something unexpected happened.

Meanwhile, the guy in the car started tearing up the

inside of the vehicle by punching the dash over and over again and ripping the radio out of its back bracket on the center console. I turned on my emergency equipment to conduct a stop. When he saw the lights, he pushed down hard on the gas pedal and burned out through the red light; the chase was on. He was going about 50 in a 30-mph zone, jumping over two sets of railroad tracks, as sparks were flying from the bottom of the car hitting the tracks. I called out the chase over the air just as I noticed a sharp turn coming up. I slowed down to see him attempt to make it, but the turn was too sharp for the speed he was going and he slid straight into a ditch, crashing the vehicle, and leaving him unable to drive any longer.

The man jumped out of the car and started running away from the crash. As I finished calling in where the crash occurred, I watched him run away on the sidewalk. I cleared the crash and drove up next to him, who by now was trotting along on the sidewalk. He had to be very drunk because if he really wanted to get away, he could have run into the woods nearby, but he chose to stay on the sidewalk. After following him for a good two blocks, I got out of my car and ran after him with my Taser already out and ready in case he wanted to fight. As I got closer to him, he stopped and decided he wanted to charge at me, yelling, "Well let's go motherfucker!"

His fists were balled up and he was ready to pounce. I quickly raised the Taser and shot him in the chest; he immediately went down. I jumped on him, wrestling his arms behind his back, and placed handcuffs on him as quickly as I could. I had to stay on top of him until my back-up arrived because of his violent and erratic behavior. They were there seconds after I handcuffed the man.

On the way to the jail, he broke down and cried the entire way there. He told me he was on cocaine and Xanax bars and didn't remember why he got arrested or why I tasered him, or why there was a police chase. He was out of it.

I can honestly say that Tasers help policing in a huge way. I believe this because we periodically run across people who are extremely high on some hard-core drugs, or they are mixing uppers and downers, like this guy. When they do this, they do not respond to pain or commands, which leaves us no choice but to fight them or Taser them. Using the Taser gives an officer time to gain control of the situation and to handcuff or detain the suspect until help arrives- whichever is more appropriate to that particular situation.

Chapter 3:
Dealing With the Mentally Ill

Paying attention to the mental health of those around us is something that needs to be done regularly in society. After all, being our brother's keeper is still a humane thing to do. Whether we like it or not, we rub off on one another more than we might think. Dealing with the mentally ill during a crisis can be tricky and every word counts. This is why as police officers we need all the training we can get our hands on. This will give us the best chance to de-escalate every potentially dangerous situation and have everyone able to go home at the end of the shift. Having the right resources in our communities at your disposal is a key part of patient recovery.

A Mentally Ill Mother

Early on in my career I received a call about a loud noise disturbance as I was patrolling the East End of Houston one night. One of the occupants of the apartment called and reported that he heard screaming inside the upstairs apartment. I could see that it was a small apartment on top of the garage, and I made my way up the rotted staircase, feeling like I was going to fall through it with every step I took leading to the front door.

Right then I heard a woman screaming, "Help me stop!" She was yelling as I ran to reach the door to her apartment, which was slightly cracked open. I pushed it open, yelling, "Police! Are you okay ma'am!?"

As I opened the door, I saw a young woman in her twenties sitting in the middle of the living room with a small infant in her right arm and a huge kitchen knife in her left hand. She was screaming and rocking nervously back and forth as she held the knife up, near the baby. All I could think about was the safety of the baby. I quickly pulled out my gun and held it behind my back, in case she made a movement toward the baby. I tried to get her to put the knife down. I quickly realized she was hearing voices and responding to them by her constant head movements and her eyes wandering around the room.

I also realized I didn't have a shot to take, because the baby was in the way. I bumped for a supervisor and a female unit to come by my scene, and both arrived quickly. While I was briefing them on what was going on, I had my eyes locked on the lady with the knife and baby. After the female officer heard what was going on, she immediately engaged in conversation with the woman, trying to get her comfortable enough to speak to her. At the time, she had only been in the department for about a year, and she impressed me on how professional she handled the situation and took charge. She connected with the woman in a way I could not. Being a mother herself and a female, she was able to quickly build a rapport with this distraught mother.

While the officer was talking to the woman, I was able to move to the opposite side of the room without her noticing. I waited until she was comfortable, and she lowered her hand that had the knife just enough for me to rush her, knocking her on her side while grabbing her left wrist that held the knife. The female officer quickly helped grab the baby while the sergeant helped me hold the lady down, who by then was screaming and trying to pull away yelling, "I'm going to kill you if you touch my baby! Don't take my baby away!"

After I wrestled the knife away from her and put her arms behind her back to handcuff her, we made sure the baby was safe.

No injuries were done to the woman who was obviously going through a mental crisis. I was definitely impressed with the new officer and I told her she did a great job. I called CPS to have them send someone to get the child, and I took the mother to the hospital where she received the medication and treatment she needed. I didn't charge her for anything because in my opinion, she needed help, and charging her would not help her in any way. I called the district attorney and she agreed as well.

How that situation turned out that day helped to cement my belief in female police officers being capable of and doing as much great work as the male officers could. So to all the people who argue that women shouldn't be police officers, I disagree 100 percent. Some of the best police officers that I have had the privilege of working with have been women.

A Suicidal Teen

It was October and just starting to cool off from the 100-degree days that are normal for Houston. I remember thinking to myself, "finally, I won't get drenched in sweat for at least these next two months." We just had roll call, where we learned that there were a series of robberies happening in different parts of the district. We were told to be on the lookout for some young Hispanic males, but no pictures were provided. That really wasn't helpful, as the area we patrolled was a predominantly Hispanic neighborhood.

After loading up my patrol car, I received notice of a major accident located in the avenues and was told there were injured people that were also fighting each other on the scene. I rushed over there and as I got closer, I could see what seemed like around 15 people fighting in a poorly lit narrow street. I also saw about six cars that were blocking the road, all with major visible damages to them. I called for backup and started to break up the fighting and separating people.

After other officers arrived, we learned that the accident was caused by two drunk drivers who were racing down the narrow street, hitting cars that were parked on the side of the road. No one was injured, but the two of them were arrested for DWI. A few officers who were in training took them to jail shortly after we had dispersed everyone from the scene and took over the accident reports.

As I was walking back to my patrol car, an older Hispanic lady started yelling for help from the balcony of her home off the side road. She ran out of her house, down the steps, and through her yard toward us. After calming her down, she told us that her son wanted to kill himself. She said he grabbed a knife from the kitchen, cut himself on his wrist, then ran into his room and locked the door.

A sergeant, two other officers and I ran toward the small two-bedroom home. As we ran into the house, I saw that it was completely trashed, as if someone wrecked it in a rage. His mother pointed us to the old wooden door and yelled, "He's in there! He already hurt himself! Please help!"

Our sergeant called out to the boy and there was no answer. Fearing that he hurt himself even more, one of the officers kicked in the door. While the other officers had their tasers out, I had my gun out just in case he decided to use us to commit suicide by charging us with the knife. As the door was kicked open, we saw the scared teenager kneeling on the floor near his bed with a kitchen knife pointed directly at his chest. He had blood all over his shirt and arms; there were also cuts on his wrists in an attempt to commit suicide. He was losing a lot of blood, so we knew we didn't have much time to take action.

After our sergeant spoke with him for about two minutes, he lowered the knife for a split second. We took the opportunity to rush him, tackling him to the ground and wrestling to get the knife from his hand. Once we defused the situation, we learned that his girlfriend cheated on him with one of his best friends. I grabbed a shirt off the floor from a pile of what looked like dirty clothes, wrapped the laceration on his arm, and applied pressure to it as we walked him outside and into the ambulance where he lay there, crying his eyes out. I just stared at him, wondering why he would want to end his young life over a girl.

We gave his mother all the information to get her boy the counseling help he needed. When I got back in my patrol car, I started thinking about what would have happened if the boy had charged us with the knife. How would I have responded? Situations like these are scary for everyone involved, and when they turn out bad with someone getting hurt or killed, it leaves officers with more questions than answers.

These are the type of situations where prompt police intervention helps to save a life and save the loved ones the horror of grieving over the death of a child.

Work-Date

I once dated a cop from another city who wanted to do a ride-along with me to see how the big city was. At first, I was quite hesitant as Houston shifts are a lot busier than the shifts she was used to. It is a bigger city with a lot more action. After her steadily asking about it for about two weeks, I finally agreed. I set it up for a Saturday during my night shift. She was excited because she said her city was so boring to patrol, it was a suburb of Houston. That Saturday, we drove up to the station together, and I introduced her to my colleagues who made it clear to me in that weird officer kind of humor that they were attracted to her- we were in a room filled with men waiting to flirt. I couldn't help but to laugh at the reactions.

I got her a radio to carry during the shift, and we sat through roll call together so that she could hear about possible suspects in certain areas around our beats. On our way out to our patrol car, I told her that it was going to be a busy night, especially around the Hispanic clubs, as they always are on Saturday nights. She seemed excited.

Our first call was a fight outside of a cantina between two guys over a working girl whose man was too drunk to even walk inside the club. These guys beat each other up pretty bad, but no weapons were used so I cuffed both of them and took them to jail for a class C misdemeanor which is the lowest charge you can put on a person. On the way to the jail, she asked why I didn't charge one of them with the higher assault charge because of the visible injuries, and I had to explain to her that both men were willingly engaging in the fight. Since no serious injuries occurred, we were just going to let them sleep it off tonight in the city jail in hopes that they would learn their lesson and be able to go to work the next week.

After booking them in jail, we started back to our district. In the patrol car, our dispatcher was incessantly putting out calls over the radio, and my partner couldn't believe how busy we were. We took a family disturbance call that dropped near where we were. I told her that while I was making contact with the complainant, she needed to observe the surroundings and let me know if there was a safety hazard that I needed to deal with. As we pulled up to the house, we noticed a very poorly lit trailer that was in the backyard of the main house.

We heard screams from inside and immediately made our way to the back of the main house. The door to the trailer was wide open. We made it known that we were there by yelling, "Police! We're coming in!" By this time, two other units pulled up and started walking toward us to back us up. The front door led immediately into the kitchen, and as we entered the house, I saw a young man in his early twenties pacing back and forth, breathing heavily and clearly in crisis. I could hear a woman's voice coming from across the house in the living room and soon found out that it was the young man's mother. I had my partner speak to her while I tried to calm down the young man who seemed to be very anxious, scared, and aggressive all at the same time. As I was trying to get his attention, he was pacing back and forth very fast. I asked him if he was on medication and he responded by yelling back at me, "I ran out of my medication two weeks ago!" I then asked him what he was diagnosed with and he yelled, "Schizophrenia and I'm bipolar! Why?! You gonna kill me?!"

I replied "No sir, we are here to help get things under control and get you help, would you want that?" No response. As the other officers were walking in, I quickly let them know his diagnosis and that he was off his meds. I then turned my focus back to the young man. As I was trying to get information as to why he was so angry, he started walking toward the counter and my partner quickly yelled at me " there's a knife set right there near him!" I told him to step away from the counter and to come speak to us in the living room, but he immediately went for a knife.

I warned him to drop the knife while I was pulling out my gun, just in case he charged us. Before I could warn him for the second time, one of the officers backing us up tasered him and he fell to the floor kicking and screaming. I put my gun back in the holster, flipped him on his stomach and pulled his arms behind his back, grabbed the knife from his hand, and handed it to one of the officers nearby. After I placed handcuffs on him, we stood him up and he was crying uncontrollably, saying he was sorry over and over again and that, "they" are trying to kill him. I asked who "they" were and he said, "People are trying to kill me every day and nobody believes me!"

I walked him to my patrol car and asked my partner to get all the information from his mother and what kind of medications that he has, so we can write it in the report when we take him to the mental facility. One of the other officers volunteered to transport him to the hospital where a health professional could evaluate him and get him the help he needed. We placed him in his backseat after a thorough search for any other weapons. I called the officer that was transporting him after he left for the hospital to get more information from him to finish the report. In the end, no charges were filed against him.

As I was writing my report, my partner was surprised at how busy we were and how many calls were still coming through, including calls still holding for us to run. As I was congratulating her on a good job with warming me about the knife, we had a call dropped on us in the avenues of a man down. Pulling up to the call, we could see an abandoned home. I noticed it was very dark, and a few people were standing outside. None of them wanted to get involved, so they all dispersed quickly. We walked up to the porch and through the window I saw a man squirming around on the floor, with foam coming out of his mouth. I got on the radio and let dispatch know what was going on and that I was about to kick in the door. I asked my partner if she wanted to kick it in so I could put my rubber gloves and be ready to help this guy. With one swift kick, the door flew open- I was definitely impressed. We rushed in and I turned him on his side and told my partner to clear the house to make sure no one else was in there. I swept his mouth with my fingers, pulled his tongue out of his throat, and took the heroin needle out of his arm. The man started catching his breath but was still struggling to breathe. The ambulance arrived shortly after and took him to the hospital for detox.

My partner asked a few questions about what happened, and then I complimented her on that awesome kick that opened the door. Even though it was an old home, I was still impressed with her kick.

Life Saving Award

As I was finishing up the report, one of my fellow officers got on the radio stating that he had a suspect in custody while a man across the street from him was screaming for help, saying his daughter was not breathing. I quickly volunteered for the call because we were only two blocks away from the incident. On the way there, I told my partner to make sure that if there's a crowd of people there to keep them away while I see what's going on with his daughter, to which she agreed nervously.

As we drove up, I noticed it was outside of a cantina that was closing down for the night. I got out of my patrol car to approach the father who was breathing heavily and visibly frightened. He told me she was 13 years old and she stopped breathing because she was choking on something. I immediately observed the little girl to be over 200 pounds and her face was pale and purple with a shade of yellow around her neck.

This girl was unconscious and not breathing, but still had a pulse. I quickly told dispatch to give me a time check because I was starting the Heimlich maneuver on her. The girl was big; I had to lean her out of the van. She was leaning onto me and I instructed her dad to hit my fist that I placed just under the breastbone every time I counted to three. Her dad eagerly stepped up to help his baby girl. After about six minutes, which felt like 20 minutes, I could feel the girl slowly gasping for air and on the last three counts, her father, who was in front of her hitting my hand, yelled at me that a big piece of meat fell out of her mouth. She was beginning to gasp for air and the color was slowly coming back to her face and throat.

I told dispatch to give me a time check, stating that she started breathing again. Time checks are very important, especially when an officer is dealing with a juvenile. You never know what might come later, sometimes we get complaints. Keeping detailed records will save you every time.

By now, the father went crazy yelling, "Thank you Lord!" and telling me, "You saved my daughter!" The ambulance drove up to check her vitals and told us she was cleared to go home and that everything seemed okay with her. My sergeant got there and by the time he got to me, he had learned from four other people what occurred. He shook my hand and told me I did an outstanding job and that he was submitting my name for a lifesaving award.

I was still trying to catch my breath from the physical and mental exertion that just took place. Concentrating on saving the life of another person creates an intensity that runs through you. My partner started crying quietly. She told me that she would never forget tonight and loved what had just happened. She asked me why I went for six minutes and I told her that our job is not to give up but to keep doing it until the ambulance gets there. Otherwise, you will live with the guilt of a lost life knowing you didn't give it everything you've got.

Chapter 4:
Chaos During Hurricane Seasons

Hurricane Ike

When in close proximity to damaging events such as the ones officers face doing their jobs, it is crazy how the mind tricks them into seeing similar situations in dreams or flashbacks. Some end up finding themselves traumatized by these events. Some end trying to break off the chain by ending their own life so that their thoughts and visions will end, and others find solace in addictions or abuse until they degenerate themselves.

One other incident which rocked my perception of humanity was a rape of a minor that happened in 2008. That year, Houston felt the power of hurricane Ike, which killed 84 people and caused $19.3 billion in damages. Hurricane Ike first hit the island of Galveston which is only 30 to 35 minutes south of Houston. Over 2.5 million people were forced to be without electricity. My apartment in the southeast side of Houston was also affected. During this time, I was forced to live at the station until my power came back on which took about a week and a half. The entire east end of Houston was without power and most homes were powered by generators running all day and night.

When natural disasters occur, it creates an opportunity for criminals to play their trade without being stopped. Looters and burglars seize the opportunity to break into property and stock up just because law enforcement officers are not on an around the clock watch during disasters. Desperate people will also break into stores and steal valuable or useful items. Aside from the fact that officers will most likely have problems of their own to sort through during this time, we will also stay busy keeping order.

Sometimes, cars would be set on fire just to cause distractions. We would catch people on rooftops trying to get into stores and malls. Some were eventually caught and taken to jail. During this time, it was standard practice to ride with a partner for safety reasons until everything cleared up on the streets. I was paired up with an officer who served in the army and just graduated from the police academy and the Field Training Officer (FTO) training program. We actually got along very well. He was the only person I didn't mind getting partnered up with during that time partly because of his similar military background and shit talking. We caught some robbery suspects, and also handled a few domestic disturbance calls together.

One night we spotted a vehicle swerving to stay in his lane, so we pulled him over to check him out. When speaking to the man, he seemed really nervous, so I decided to run him through the system and his name came back with ten different warrants for his arrest. My partner arrested him for the warrants and had a wrecker hook up his vehicle to get towed. As I was filling out the paperwork for the wrecker, a very young girl of about seven years old walked up to me from the neighborhood directly behind the store where we were pulled over. She said "hi" and I turned around and saw her standing next to me in a dirty and torn white dress that looked a dingy gray from the dirt.

I said to her, "Yes ma'am. What can I do for you?" She was crying a little, but could speak clearly and said "my neighbor told me to go to flashing lights if I was ever in trouble". I said, "Well that's great. I'm glad she told you that- are you okay?" She said. "Yes, but my sister..." She couldn't find the words to finish.

I asked, "Why? Where is she?" She said, "She's at home." She paused for a moment, and then she found a way to tell me "I think my mom's boyfriend is touching my sister the wrong way".

My heart dropped. I picked her up onto the hood of my patrol car and asked her if he was touching her right then, and she nodded her head. Then she said, "I'm scared." I asked her how she got here and she replied, "I heard my sister screaming, so I ran outside and saw your lights." I asked her if she knew where her house was, and she nodded as tears started running down her face. I quickly called my partner over to brief him on what was going on and you could immediately see the emotion flow through his face. My partner had small children at home- I didn't.

I got on the radio and called for another unit, along with the sergeant, to meet us. I briefed them both and the officer agreed to take our prisoner to jail after telling the sergeant what was going on. He asked the girl, "Can you take us to your house?" She immediately said, "Yes" as her tears began to dry.

As we followed her, I told my partner to wait in the back of the house in case the suspect ran out the back exit. I proceeded to check out the front entrance. I noticed that the apartment was situated on the top of a garage with a balcony wrapped around it and a narrow staircase on the left side of the garage leading up to the apartment.

On the way up the stairs, I could hear generators from all the surrounding homes drowning out any other noises as I worked my way to the window, flashing my flashlight into each room. Once I got around the balcony, I could see that each room was empty and messy. I flashed the light in the second to the last room from the back and saw the man thrusting himself into this small scared girl. I could barely hear her screaming over the loud generators. I quickly used my flashlight to break the window and rushed in as fast as I could. As soon as the glass broke, he picked up his sweatpants and bolted out the back door. I got on the radio to warn my partner that he was on his way back toward him. He jumped over the fence right into the arms of my pissed off partner who was waiting for him. When I met up with them in the backyard, he was struggling with the suspect, until we were able to very gently place him in handcuffs and put him in the backseat.

It is in these moments you wish you could have a few minutes alone with the suspect, but remembering that we have to be professional at all times matters. I called for an ambulance to check him and the little girl who was still crying by herself in the room. She was taken to the hospital straight away. A few minutes after we got the guy into custody, the girl's mother showed up yelling and cursing at us for arresting her man.

My sergeant learned that she knew what was going on but she defended herself and her man, claiming that her little girls always flirted with him so it was not his fault. We arrested her because she knew about it and did not do anything to stop it.

The biggest twist to the story happened moments after we had arrested all of the suspects and finished the necessary paperwork. A white work van slid to a stop next to our patrol cars and a hysterical Hispanic male got out with a baseball bat, running straight toward us. Officers drew their pistols and yelled at him to drop the bat and the man stopped quickly. We heard the little girl that saved her sister call out to him "Daddy!" while crying. It was the biological father coming to help his kids. We explained to him what had happened and what charges we were going to file on both the mother and boyfriend.

The father's face dropped and my heart hurt for him because he had absolutely no clue that this was going on for over a year. My partner and I took the kids to the juvenile division where the investigators took video statements from them. Their father met us up there and we let him take the kids home after they were done. Their father thanked us over and over again, blaming himself for everything that happened. He was crying and was obviously in emotional pain. We told him that it wasn't his fault and that the girls needed him to be strong for them. We also advised him to take them to a counselor as soon as possible.

My partner and I didn't say a word the whole drive back to the station. Neither of us could grasp what we just had to handle. We unpacked the patrol car, putting our gear in our own personal vehicles. As we gave each other fist bumps to say goodbye, I asked him "you good?" knowing he was bothered more than I was about the scene we just witnessed. He replied "I gotta go see my kids man." I could see the hurt in his eyes before he turned away and walked to his car.

I got home that night both physically and mentally drained. I couldn't get the visual of the man trying to thrust into the little girl out of my head. To this day, I have my moments about that incident. In a way I was glad that I was the one who saw that and not my partner because I know he would have taken that harder with him having children of his own. You may not realize this, but cops live with things they see and experience in the streets. Some cops turn to alcohol as a means to forget, while some become even better people, choosing to focus on the positives and rise from the gloom. Either way it changes them.

Heavy Rains

One night when I was starting my shift, we had a storm coming in which meant most likely we would have quite a few accidents on the freeways. As the night began, the rain was pouring down so heavily it almost seemed angry. I loaded all my gear in my patrol car and was soaking wet by the time I finally got into my seat. The rain was not supposed to let up all night and there were accidents already dropping over the radio for us to respond to in different areas of our district. I volunteered for a minor accident and handled it quickly because there was just one car involved. It spun out on the freeway and hit the median, leaving it stranded and blocking two lanes. After making sure the driver was okay, I had the wrecker tow it since it was not drivable.

The driver had someone coming to pick her up. As I was finishing the report in my patrol car, another accident dropped near me, so I took it and started down the freeway while the wrecker driver stayed with the woman until her ride arrived. While I was driving, I noticed the rain picked up even more, making it very hard to see in front of me. I began to drive slowly in fear that I was going to hit something. After about five minutes, I could see the lights from a wrecker and a stalled out vehicle. I noticed that the entire wheel flew off a small vehicle and landed in the middle of the highway, leaving the vehicle stalled in the middle of the freeway. I put my emergency lights on so people could see us. The wrecker driver quickly hooked up the car and towed it off the highway onto the right shoulder where it was safe. It soon stopped raining, but was super dark with very little light as a thick fog was beginning to form.

As I was getting all the information from the vehicle, I heard the wrecker driver yell out, "Hey, I'm getting the tire out of the street so no one gets into an accident later!" Before I could say anything, I heard a loud screeching sound and then a loud "bang." It was the wrecker driver being hit. A black van was traveling down the dark highway and didn't see him until the last second. I saw a big man step out of the van yelling at me, "I hit him! Where is he?!" I called for more units to help, and after 10 minutes of looking, we found his lifeless body about 20 yards from the freeway in the grass with a huge piece of the van's windshield sticking out of his chest.

As I was walking back to my patrol car to call it in to our dispatch, I looked at the wrecker truck and saw a small boy who looked to be no more than 10 years old, staring in the direction of his Dad's body. He was in complete shock and his eyes were filled with tears. I managed to run over to the boy and held him tight as he wept. I was able to contact his mother and she soon showed up. The woman was hysterical herself and I quickly explained to her what happened and that her son saw everything and he needs her to be strong for him. She grabbed the boy and hugged him while I got her information written down so I could release the boy to her. It was a crazy night.

The medical examiner picked up the body and after they left, we cleared the scene and I sat in my patrol car feeling bad for the child. I could not imagine seeing my Dad get killed in front of me. This reminded me of when my old man ran into the burning apartment in front of me. We were both just ten years old when these incidents occurred, but his story unfortunately did not have the same outcome as mine.

The other officers attended to the man who hit the wrecker driver because he was very shaken up too. We learned that he was on his way to work and didn't see the wrecker driver until it was too late to react. The man was let go for the moment because we felt he honestly couldn't see the man due to the darkness and heavy fog. I could definitely tell that the man was suffering from the thoughts of killing another man. He was crying and kept asking about the young boy we took out of the wrecker.

There was no doubt that the son and the man that struck his Dad definitely suffered trauma. I remember hoping that they would get the help they both needed. In the end, it is often better not to get involved too deeply in the traumatic side of things because the experience is torturing. While it is helpful to be able to disconnect from these stories, sometimes there's no way you can.

Hurricane Harvey

During the hurricanes, officers are never in doubt that there will be an increase in calls in their district. On August 25, 2017 Hurricane Harvey hit the Houston area. It not only left behind a trail of massive flooding but also over 60 confirmed deaths, one of whom was a Houston Police Sergeant. He died while trying to get to his station to help his fellow officers save the lives of Houstonians. He got caught in high waters which ended up taking his life. Ultimately, he died a hero by thinking of others and choosing not to stay at home that day.

This level of flooding had not been witnessed in recent times. The water damaged thousands of homes and left thousands more homeless and living in shelters around Houston. This hurricane consisted mainly of heavy rainfall, while Hurricane Ike that hit Houston in 2008 had very strong winds that knocked out power all over the city. Harvey dripped constant rainfall for days. With no winds in most of the city and nowhere for the water to drain to, water levels rose quickly. Homes and vehicles were flooded throughout the city, including areas that have never seen flooding ever before.

The day before the hurricane hit, many people stayed in the city because the mayor had said on television that we were not expected to get a lot of damage or flooding – so we were somewhat reassured. I didn't prepare for much at all, my wife stocked the house with about four days worth of food. I got two emergency cases of water for the house, just in case she was stuck there for a few more days. On my part, I bought a few days worth of food and drinks for the office, knowing we were going to be riding out the storm at work.

Of course, all officers had to be at work at these crucial times, so we packed for a few days. That Thursday evening, I worked an extra job for a construction company, closing off lanes as they worked overnight. After that job, I went straight to work for my regular shift. During the day, it started raining by mid-morning with a constant flow of rain, gradually pouring down harder and harder as the day went on. We were put on 16-hour shifts as the rain picked up and you could tell by the intensity of the rain that there was going to be a lot of flooding.

The first few hours we were there, we served on the food lines and helped cook in the back of the Police Union. After a few more hours, they were asking if anyone had a truck to pick up more supplies at a restaurant depot and I quickly volunteered to get away from the somewhat boring and passive position I found myself in.

I had access to a big, jacked up flatbed truck that was assigned to the property division, so I drove it to the union where we were meeting up to follow each other in case anyone flooded out. We made our way through the streets to the store where we stocked up the entire flatbed truck with sodas and water. As we were loading, we were getting drenched because the rain was relentless. It never stopped.

While we were there, my supervisor called us back to our station. He wanted us to report to the shelters because they were funneling people in. We hurried back, unloaded the truck in the pouring rain, and headed back to our station where we changed out of our soaking wet clothes and prepared for our next assignment. We were able to rest for about four hours and then had to report to the George R. Brown Convention Center, which had been converted into a massive shelter. Many had to abandon their homes already. Although the flood hadn't seriously affected my house yet, I still worried about my family.

The George R. Brown Convention Center sheltered over ten thousand people when it first opened up to the community. There were families seeking shelter and coming in straight from being rescued by some of the bravest people I have seen.

While we were dealing with people flowing into the shelters, police officers, The National Guard, and civilians who volunteered to help with their personal boats, were conducting the most amazing rescues all throughout the city and surrounding areas. I soon realized the police couldn't have handled something so large-scale without the involvement of all these other volunteers. While this storm brought in many people who actually needed what was being offered, it also brought in others who took full advantage of the free stuff being handed out.

During my very first day at the shelter, I got out of the police van and saw a long line of people that wrapped around our 46-acre convention center. There were so many families with small infants and also animals. My heart dropped knowing that a lot of them lost everything they worked their whole lives for. They had no other option but to be here at the shelter. As I walked inside, I saw officers I knew searching people for contraband such as weapons and drugs while families filed in, one by one.

The atmosphere was very chaotic. Some people were crying and visibly sad, some were scared, and some prayed for relief. They huddled together in corners along the walls for warmth and support. I saw a few people I arrested before walking around in there as well. Knowing they may still be on probation, I made a quick connection with them to let them know to behave in there, because we would not think twice about throwing them out and banning them from the shelter if they misbehaved or tried to take advantage of the situation.

This hurricane was a surprise to most, so we made adjustments as we took people in. Everyone was put in pods that held around three to four thousand people and they were all mixed up together, which caused a lot of tension and drama between families and single men and women. There were also many people who were criminals of all kinds stuck in the same shelter as families. The police tried very hard to have enough officers in the sleeping quarters, making sure no one was sexually assaulted or robbed. Trying to manage this was no small feat.

The real excitement was outside of the shelter where people were allowed to smoke cigarettes and walk around all night. We had many people taking advantage and sneaking paraphernalia into the huge smoking area. Some were smoking Kush - a synthetic drug made of all kinds of hazardous chemicals. They smoke this by rolling it in a cigarette or a cigar and a lot of them would overdose. They often fell to the floor from the high - hitting their heads and causing lacerations or head trauma. Some would have seizures and foam at the mouth, flopping around on the floor until we arrived to turn them on their sides so they did not choke on their tongues. We would call for EMS to come get them and we helped them when they arrived. The ones that did not overdose were walking around like zombies, slowly dragging their feet with very slow response times. They were also slurring their words and did not know where they were.

We came to the conclusion that the only way we can have things calm down in the shelter is if we start kicking out people who are taking advantage of what the shelter has to offer - especially the ones who were smoking and trying to get high around the kids that were in the shelter. After the sixth day of nothing but overdoses day and night, the Red Cross workers started getting really agitated and yelling at them all the time when they were clearly high as a kite. Finally, they gave us the green light to start kicking people out.

After we got a lot of the troublemakers out, everything was really calm and the people there were very appreciative of how we handled things. It was heartbreaking to see people pouring into the shelters, knowing they lost everything that they had worked for, yet trying to keep their hopes high. During my shifts, I had a lot of time to speak to many of the people who lost everything. They would talk about their stories, as if their entire lives flashed in front of them. It was tough for me to hear about all the devastation. I spoke to one elderly man who told me that he was in his wheelchair in chest-deep water with his two grandchildren, both under ten years old, standing on the arms of the wheelchair while the water was slowly rising. He said that he couldn't move at all and was thinking that they were going to die when a boat pulled up after hearing their cries for help. He said that it was still raining pretty hard outside when the three guys broke his window and swam through it to pull them out of the house the same way the men got there- through the window. This man lost everything and as he was telling me the story, he had tears in his eyes. I felt a deep pain for him and his family in my heart.

While in the shelter, we would have some people who were originally homeless also causing problems every now and then, but after the first two weeks, it began running more smoothly. A few other officers and I would play football or soccer with the small kids in the shelter to help time pass by quickly. I will say that some of the kids did not like cops and it was obvious when they shied away from us when we tried to interact with them. However, after spending time together day in and day out, they seemed to have changed their mindset about us and would often yell our names and give us fist bumps. In a way, this disaster helped us reach out to a lot of the youth. Hopefully this gave them a different view of officers as the ones who not only keep society safe and running smoothly, but we are also there to help them lead better lives. Spending time with our communities I think is the key to healing society as a whole.

Chapter 5:
Fighting False Accusations

Falsely Accused

One night in 2008 I conducted a traffic stop in the Southside of Houston just after midnight. I pulled up to this particular car because he was parked in the middle of an intersection and I assumed he was having a problem with his vehicle. I lit him up with the spotlight from my patrol vehicle, and the driver behind the wheel made a movement toward the passenger side of his truck. I immediately activated my emergency lights so I could conduct a traffic stop, and in doing so, the driver abruptly accelerated his vehicle, causing his wheels to spin and screech as he peeled out of the intersection and pulled halfway into his mother's driveway, about two houses from the corner. I did not notify dispatch because I didn't have a chance to with such a short chase.

I approached the truck by the driver's side, and yelled for him to step out of the vehicle with my gun drawn. When he got out and I saw he was an older man with a calm demeanor, I put my weapon back in my holster. I asked him why he didn't pull over when I put my lights on him and he said, "I didn't want you to arrest me." And I said, "Why would I arrest you? Do you have warrants?" He then said, "I'm clean, brother."

I ran the man via MDT in the patrol vehicle after observing a valid insurance card and Texas driver's license. The background check came back with multiple city warrants. By this time, two officers checked by with me. It was a training unit, and I asked the officers if they wanted the arrest for training. The officer in charge, who was my academy classmate, agreed to take him. I briefed him on what had occurred before they got there and also let them know he had several city warrants.

The more experienced officer told his partner to get the suspect out of the vehicle and place him under arrest for his warrants. While the unit was taking control of the suspect, we were confronted by two individuals who identified themselves as the suspect's son and mother; both of them remained behind a closed fence. The mother seemed to be very calm and was trying to get information as to where the suspect would be taken. While this was going on, her other son (the one not under arrest) kept interrupting his mother, and yelling at me, "You're a racist motherfucker! I always see you around here arresting Black people in the neighborhood. Do you know who we are? I will have your badge by the end of the week. What's your badge number and name?"

The transporting officers were placing the suspect in the patrol vehicle so I assumed that his comments were directed toward me. I provided the suspect's son with my badge number and my name, which he wrote down on a piece of paper. Then his mother asked me if he could keep his vehicle where it was. I told her that I would have to ask the suspect to get his permission to release the vehicle to her. By now, the suspect was in the back of a patrol car getting ready to be transported to jail. Unfortunately for his mother, he refused to speak to me. His car ended up getting towed and the officers took off to the jail.

After my shift, one of the officers who transported the suspect called me to say that the suspect had a seizure in the back seat when they were pulling into the jail. He told me that he started foaming at the mouth and they had to turn him on his side before the ambulance came to pick him up and took him to the hospital. I told him to make sure he writes down what happened, just in case a complaint is filed. I hung the phone up starting to feel bad about the officers having to deal with that when that was actually my call.

I went home, took a shower, and went straight to bed. Four hours into my sleep, I received a call from a sergeant from our internal affairs telling me to get up and report to his office immediately. I asked him what this was all about and the sergeant said, "You know what it is about." I actually didn't know so that bothered me. It was obvious that the sergeant was mad, and I had no idea what was going on. The drive to internal affairs was unsettling. I kept trying to think of stuff I might have screwed up, but I couldn't come up with anything. I was worried.

When I got there I checked in at the front desk and got a very nasty look from the secretary, who was watching Maury on TV. After waiting about 15 minutes, the sergeant finally appeared and brought me back to his office. His demeanor was clear: I was definitely in trouble. He asked me for my credentials and I gave them to him. At this point I was curious and upset.

I said, "Yes, sir. Can I know what this is all about?"

He looked me straight in the eye and said, "Don't play dumb! Get out of my office!"

I had absolutely no idea what was going on until I got back into my car and received a call from the other officer who transported the suspect the night before. He said they also took his badge, along with his rookie's badge. He was just as confused as I was.

When I got home a few days later and turned on the television, I was surprised to see the suspect from the night before on the local News – standing outside his mother's porch in a brand-new suit, giving a full-blown press conference. Standing next to him was a local activist from the Houston area. They were going on and on about his arrest and how he was beat up by the police. My mouth dropped. I was not questioned about what happened during the incident before they took my badge away. I immediately called my union representatives, and they came to my aid quickly. Honestly, without these people standing up for me, I don't know how I would still have this beautiful job today. I literally owe my career to the Houston Police Union's legal team and our union leader for standing up for me.

The activist gave press conferences on how brutal I and the other two officers were. It was horrible to watch and we couldn't even defend ourselves from the crazy accusations because we couldn't make any statements while the investigation was ongoing. You can probably imagine how that set in with the public.

They were protesting in front of the courthouse with signs

that had my full name all over them, ruining my reputation more and more with each protest that was held.

Finally, our union leader had enough and held a press conference with all three of us there, next to our two attorneys. My lawyer called out the media and also called out our higher-ups for the way they handled the situation.

The city had a field day with this story while we waited five months for a grand jury hearing. I had to hear family and friends speak very negatively about the three of us, and how they believed we handled ourselves that night.

You know, you don't see who is there for you and who loves you until you experience an event like what we went through. To sit there and listen to the slandering of our names and characters is a hard thing to do, knowing that all of this was false and that all we could do was wait our turn. After months of waiting, I finally got to tell my story in front of the grand jury. I was nervous because I have never had to testify in front of the grand jury before. This was a serious event in my life and something I will never forget. I can remember sitting outside of the door in a chair, waiting to go in and wondering if this was the last day I would be able to wear my uniform. My heart was pounding out of my chest.

As I walked into the room I sat at a podium in front of about 12 people at a huge horseshoe shaped desk. I noticed that the people I would be talking to were very diverse, which made me feel at ease a little. I knew I had a solid, honest case. To be right and to be nervous doesn't make sense, but as soon as the words left my mouth, I knew that I would be found innocent.

Before the hearing, I went down and had evidence pulled

from that night that was hard evidence (which I cannot list in this book) that cleared me from any wrongdoing. The suspect claimed that I pulled into the back of a gas station, beat him up, and made him swallow crack rocks that he tested positive for when he was in the hospital. This evidence showed I was nowhere near a gas station at all.

I presented this information to the grand jury with such confidence that at the end, the grand jury walked out of the room to meet me where I was waiting, and one-by-one shook my hand and thanked me for my service.

I was cleared of all wrongdoing and I was reinstated and back on the streets doing the job that I love to do a few days later. During times like these, I have to remind myself that my job is awesome and self-fulfilling in many ways, much more than anything that threatens my position. I learned to always take notes and keep track of everything I do for these reasons. I also learned a lot about friends and family, specifically who is loyal and who is not. It is crucial in our line of work to always make notes and reports to cover your actions because you seriously don't know who will come after you.

Saved by the Dash Cam

I had another experience with a suspect who I believe had to be under the influence but turned out to just be crazy as hell. This particular incident could have destroyed my career if not for the evidential trail left by the presence of my Dash Cam videos.

Officers have to deal with a lot of stressful situations on the job. It continues throughout their career- this fact is pretty well-known around the nation. But one other thing which is not publicized are the continual false accusations made toward police officers. This close shave with false accusations almost broke me. The incident could have changed my life for the worse if not for the evidence that was in my favor.

This particular incident took place sometime during the summer break of 2012 when I was working an overtime shift for traffic enforcement. The overtime was available because of the increase in accidents on the freeway caused by aggressive driving and DUIs. Our job was to identify drivers that were possibly under the influence or just driving aggressively by following too close to other vehicles or failing to signal lane changes. Usually we are able to slow people down after they see us issuing out citations. In doing so, it saves thousands of dollars in repairs to vehicles. More importantly, it saved lives.

I was halfway through my shift driving down the freeway when I saw a small tan Nissan weaving in and out of his lane, causing the drivers around him to swerve out of their lanes to avoid hitting him. I got behind him and turned on my emergency lights, signaling him to pull to the side of the freeway. The vehicle did so immediately, which was great. When I approached the car, I observed the middle-aged man in the vehicle to be a very polite man who was calm the entire time while I explained why I pulled him over. All his responses were "Yes, sir" and "No, sir" responses. I noticed his Texas driver's license needed to be renewed so I ran him in our system and it came back with no warrants, so I wrote him a ticket for one moving violation instead of the four I could have written. I just made sure to remind him again to renew his license before letting him drive off. Then I told him to have a good day and he said the same to me.

I got back into my patrol car to fill out some paperwork needed for the traffic stop I just made when an old academy classmate of mine who worked in that area called me and told me to look up an incident number that was reported. When I pulled up the incident, I saw it was the man I just stopped and wrote a ticket to. That was interesting. As I kept reading from my computer screen, I was surprised. The man stated the following: "Officer Marin pulled me over and cursed me out, then assaulted me with his clipboard." I couldn't believe what I was reading! He also stated that he was presently at a nearby grocery store waiting for an ambulance.

I called my sergeant, briefed him on the situation and told him to meet me out there. As I pulled into the grocery store parking lot, I saw the ambulance there attending to him and I saw the other officer who called me there as well, next to him. I parked near them, and as I got out of my car the sergeant pulled up next to me and went straight over to the man, asking him questions about what happened. After about 5 minutes, my sergeant stormed over to me and asked me if I hit the man and stated that he had a large cut on his forehead that may need stitches. I was shocked. I said, "Wow! Hold on. Before you side with him, all my traffic stops are recorded with audio and video. I have a dash cam and a mic on me. Feel free to review the footage." I pointed to the small TV screen that went to the video control panel above the rear-view mirror, inside the patrol car.

His mood changed to a lighter tone as he responded, "I totally forgot you had that." As he got into the car and reviewed the video footage, he respectfully apologized to me and walked over to the man who was accusing me of wrongdoing and arrested him for making a false report on a police officer.

I am a strong supporter of video cameras and body cameras, especially if they have audio, because officers can use them for protection in a court of law. However, the downside to having cameras is that it takes away an officer's discretion on how to handle some traffic stops or certain calls.

An example of an officer's discretion during a traffic stop means that the officer can show leniency and not write a ticket. Sometimes, verbal warnings do the job. With cameras, we cannot use that discretion. The point is that with the cameras, we have to act on every infraction that we come across. As time goes on, I think that police departments are getting a little more lenient on some issues.

I would have thought that was the end of the false accusation episode but three months later, while on a call with my partner, I got a call out of the blue from the Criminal Investigation Department (CID) Unit warning me that the same man from the Dash Cam event called our dispatchers and made a threat to my life. He reportedly said, "I will shoot him when I see him!" in reference to me.

I thanked them for the heads up and they said that they were trying to find out his whereabouts to make a felony arrest for a terroristic threat to a police officer. Worried about him following me to my parent's home where my two younger brothers and sisters lived, paranoia began to set in.

In the following days, I was more aware of my surroundings and how cars drove around or near me. This was not the first time my life had been threatened as a cop, but something about this guy was off. Three days passed and I received a call from CID. They informed me that they found out where the suspect lived. When they sent two constables out to his house, the situation ended up escalating into a shootout with him. The suspect was dead and officers were okay. My emotions were in even more disarray after hearing the news of his death. On one hand, the fact that his initial encounter with me triggered his death left me with a weird feeling. On the other hand, I felt like if I had not been careful enough to avoid him I could have been the one that he encountered. This left me internally shaken for days. Fortunately I was able to sort these feelings out during counseling sessions.

Looking back at the many encounters officers have throughout our careers, we often deal with some great people. But, every now and then, we deal with evil people whose intentions toward us are impure. After years of trial and error my philosophy as a police officer is that it is always best to be careful, treat people with respect and patience first. It is also imperative to keep good notes on what occurred and keep your cameras on.

Chapter 6:
Some Memorable Incidents

Beyond the awards and accolades we get for jobs well done, other aspects of our work also give us life. As much as there are adrenaline-filled episodes in our work, there are fun moments too. Sometimes, we have our fun on outings and at other times, the fun finds us while we are at work. The fun is guaranteed for those who have at least a moderate sense of humor.

Rare Honesty

As soon as I got on the DWI Task Force, I began conducting traffic stops. On one dark and foggy night, I was driving down a main road in the East End and I saw a car swerving from one lane to the other. In response, I pulled over and waited for her to pass me. After she passed me, I made a U-Turn and called it in over the air and quickly caught up to the vehicle. I signaled for her to pull over by lighting her up with my emergency lights. The vehicle pulled over very quickly. As I approached the vehicle on the driver side I noticed the window rolled down, and heard the lady yell, "What the fuck took you so long to stop me?! I've been driving fucked up for nearly an hour now!"

I was confused, "You're right ma'am. I won't let that happen again."

To which she responded, "You better not! I could've killed someone!"

"Well ma'am. I'm glad you didn't. Can you please step out of the vehicle for me?"

After she got out of her car, I had her perform all the field sobriety tests and every time she fell to the ground and yelled, "See? I can't even stand up and I was driving!! Take me to jail, idiot!"

"Yes ma'am. Turn around please, and place your hands behind your back." My camera was rolling the entire time and I could bet the footage would be very intriguing to anyone who saw it afterward.

Oftentimes, I wish all arrests were this easy.

Driving on Rims

I have had a lot of hilarious experiences with drunk drivers. On my first training shift on nights, I was assigned to the east end of Houston near the ship channel, which is a predominantly Hispanic community. It was a Monday night, so I really wasn't expecting much action.

As I loaded up the patrol car with gear for the evening, my new trainer for the night playfully asked, "Are you ready?"

I responded jokingly, "I'm always ready!" He laughed a

little, knowing I had no idea how it was on the night shift. My trainer was an army veteran who had 10 years on the police force and still rocked the high and tight haircut from the army. To many, he came off as arrogant and mean. I, on the other hand, was used to men like him coming from the military and in many ways, I was like him, which is why we got along so well. We still keep in touch to this day.

As we pulled out of the station, we immediately got a 'fight in progress' call over our radios from dispatch. Driving the streets with lights and sirens going code-one at night had a totally different feel than it did during the day and evening shift. The adrenaline and excitement was definitely heightened for me. From that moment on, I knew my place was on the night shift.

As we got to the location, people were scattering everywhere and made it impossible to see who was fighting. The scene cleared and no one was injured, so we cleared everyone out and put ourselves back in service, ready for the next call. As we pulled away, an older Ford pick-up drove past us, throwing sparks in the air from all four tires. A Hispanic driver inside had the Tejano music blaring with his windows rolled down, and wasn't even trying to hide the beer bottle he had in his hand that he was using to steer the truck with.

My trainer and I both laughed and shook our heads at what we just witnessed. I busted a U-turn around the median and conducted a traffic stop on the vehicle. As I was calling out our location of the traffic stop to dispatch, my trainer whispered for me to look - nodding his head toward the vehicle we just pulled over to the side of the road. Both of us started laughing as we saw the driver. Through the spotlight I had pointed directly at his back window we could see the driver climbing over his center console into the passenger seat and then throwing out about five or six beer bottles into the grass near the sidewalk. I approached the vehicle on the driver's side and my trainer stayed on the passenger side. I observed the rims of the vehicle touching the concrete road with shreds of ripped tires that were barely hanging on. I asked the man what happened, and he responded, "He ran out! You didn't see him? He took off running!," he said, pointing down the street.

I had to hold back my laughter once again because he was dead serious and slurring every word. I instructed him to get out of the vehicle. My trainer, however, could not contain himself and was cracking up as he opened the passenger door. The guy stumbled out and fell on the curb, causing minor scratches from the gravel. As we helped him up, we asked him how much he had to drink and he said he only had two beers. What's funny is that two is a common number that gets thrown out at us when we ask people we suspect of being drunk. No matter how drunk they are, they always say they just had two beers.

I remember he reeked of alcohol, had glassy blood-shot eyes, and needed our assistance to stand up straight and walk. As I assisted him to our patrol car, I realized that the night shift deals with a whole different side of the public. This was my very first DWI case, and I honestly hated the entire process because it was so lengthy. Ironically, I have spent most of my career working these specific cases because of the seriousness of the offense, and also because I hated seeing children die from drunk drivers.

Later on in my career, arrests like these led me to receive a MADD award - Mothers against Drunk Driving - for the amount of DWI convictions I made over the years. This group of ladies is awesome and would sometimes bring our night shift food and drinks to our unit. I feel for these ladies because they lost children to drunk driving. I have always had all the respect in the world for them knowing they went through that and dedicated their lives fighting drunk driving and supporting those who are arresting them.

Cookies and Toys

During our lunch one day, about four of us took a break at a gas station in our district. My colleagues grabbed coffee while I grabbed a bottle of water. As we walked back outside to our patrol cars, we heard a man yelling and cursing at people walking by him in the parking lot. It was an old white man tweaking out, high on crack cocaine. I stopped to ask him what he was on and he calmly replied, "I'm high on life, man!" He was also laughing at the top of his lungs. I told him to come over to where I was and that I knew he was on something. I then asked him for his ID. He handed it over, still laughing away.

I then asked him what he had in the backpack that was on his back. And again, he started laughing and this time he said, "Cookies and toys!" After getting his permission, I opened his backpack. As I reached in to search around, I grabbed what I thought was a rubber tube of some sort, but found there were two huge veiny dildos! I placed them on the hood of my patrol car, trying to keep a straight face in the process.

I tried my best to hold back the laughter, even when I heard my three colleagues in the background cracking up and making nasty jokes about how I grabbed the dildos out of the bag and placed them on the hood of my car. When I looked in the bag again, I grabbed a hold of a huge 12-ounce bottle of lube. By then, I couldn't take it anymore and I started laughing at the absurdity of this entire situation. The man did not pay attention to me. The drugs kept his mind busy with a few hallucinations as I watched his eyes dart rapidly with the movement of his head.

With one last search in his backpack, I pulled out four huge "cookies." That's drug slang for crack rocks that are about the size of a cookie. He also had small baggies and a small scale for weighing the crack. The old man was so high he still didn't know what was going on. By this time, other officers who were with me came over and helped book the old man into jail. They got a good laugh. They couldn't stop laughing about the thought that I grabbed dildos, for the next few weeks I fell victim to endless jokes aimed at me over this.

Homeless Guy

On another slow night, my partner and I were driving through the neighborhood checking things out in the south-central district when I spotted a homeless man dancing on the median in a busy intersection. When I pulled over to investigate, I saw that he was an older black man in his late sixties and was extremely happy. I asked him to leave the median and come over to me on the side of the road and he did. When I asked where he was staying, he said he didn't know yet. Usually I am not moved by things like this, but his outlook on life and his overall attitude changed my mind after having some small talk with him.

He said he was so happy because someone gave him a bottle of water and now he could dance all night. He kept smiling at me, showing all his missing teeth and thanking me for what police do around the neighborhood. He asked me who my favorite singer of all time was and I said Michael Jackson. Growing up, I used to have a white glove and would try to do the spin and moonwalk all the time. The old man's face lit up as he said, "I know all his songs! This one is for you!" He did a quick spin and started singing Dirty Diana. I started laughing so hard because he was trying to do his moves and sing at the same time. He was really uncoordinated, catching himself a lot before tumbling to the ground a few times.

After the song, he asked me if I liked it and I said, "Man I like it so much I'm gonna hook you up!" Across the street was an inn and I told him to follow me. I left my patrol car there on the median and walked with him to the inn. He finally said, "Sir I can't go over there; they don't want me there, they got mad at me when I asked them to use their bathroom earlier." I gave a sarcastic laugh in disbelief and told him to follow me. As we walked into the lobby the lady at the front desk asked if he did something to the property, as if she was anticipating something was wrong.

I told her no and to ring up a room for the rest of the week and weekend for him. She looked at me, wanting to say something, but thought better of it, and made a key for the old man. While she was making the key, I could hear the man crying behind me. He was overwhelmed with gratitude, thanking me over and over again.

I told him to get off his feet for a few days and relax, and take a shower. I gave him $60 cash and told him to grab some food for the week and also some soap. The lady saw the man crying and I think she had a reality check with herself because she offered to give him free soap and laundry detergent.

The old man asked me why I was doing this for him and I told him that I just finished a call where a child was sexually assaulted and had to hear from a little girl how her mom's boyfriend raped her and it tore me up. I told him his attitude and the way he appreciated life helped me get my mind off of my last call. I had plummeted into a bad mood and held onto it until I ran into this man. I told him to keep his attitude the way it was and to keep smiling. He hugged me and said, "God bless you." I thanked him and said that I appreciated the praise he gave officers because it's not the norm around here anymore. Once I walked out of the hotel, I never saw that man again. I've often wondered what became of him. As a police officer working patrol, I have run into some unusual characters. I often wonder if they were placed there along my path to impact my life.

A Crappy Time

One evening, I had gotten cleared to get back to work after a shooting incident. I was working the night shift in the middle of the week and I got a call from our dispatcher about a guy who was dragging his girlfriend down the street by her hair. This was toward the middle of my shift and I was about to call out to get a bite to eat, but I took the call instead. Another officer notified dispatch that he would stop by the scene as a secondary unit.

As we made our way to the street, I immediately spotted the man. He was a middle-aged Hispanic male with a medium build. He was wearing jeans but did not have any shoes or shirt on while dragging a woman who appeared to be in her mid-twenties by her hair. She was very petite, and wearing a dress with blood all in the front. Her hair was wrapped in a bunch around his fist, while he yelled and screamed at her about cheating on him. She was repeatedly pleading for help, kicking and reaching for her hair in desperation. I drove up next to them, got out my patrol car and shouted to the man to let her go. He did not acknowledge my command, so I ran over and grabbed him. He turned to confront me, freeing the woman from his grasp so she could crawl away quickly. After a brief struggle, I was able to guide him to the ground and place handcuffs on him. My secondary unit pulled up and helped me with the arrest by placing him in his patrol car.

As we walked him to my patrol car, he cursed and kicked all the way into the backseat. He also reeked of alcohol. My secondary officer went to aid the woman who had visible wounds on her face. She was bleeding from cuts on her face and her head from where the hair was pulled out while being dragged down the street. She said she came home from a family party and was met by him in the driveway of her house, accusing her of cheating on him. Before she could open her mouth, he smacked her around and punched her, knocking her to the ground. She continued to describe how he grabbed her hair and started yanking her around the yard, dragging her to the street until I pulled him off of her.

As we were getting the woman's information for the report, we heard a loud pop from my patrol car and I ran over to see what had happened. The back window was busted out of the car in the backseat, and this guy was trying to wiggle out the window, cutting himself up by the broken glass left on the edges of where he kicked. I pulled him out of the car and had to place him in my patrol car. This time, we buckled him in where he could not climb out of the window. He was still yelling and screaming when we were finishing up with his girlfriend.

As we walked back to the patrol car to get all of the suspect's information, we could smell shit. The closer we got to the car, the stronger the smell was. When we opened the door to the backseat he was still buckled in, but he managed to crap himself and reach in his pants with his hands and scoop out as much as he could and smear it all over the plastic backseat. He was planning on us taking him out of the vehicle, but that was not going to be the case. We lowered the windows and let him sit in his mess and took him straight to jail where we booked him immediately. The smell didn't leave the patrol car even after two trips to get it detailed over the next few weeks. That drove me up the wall, so in a way he won.

A Great Man

This story is about someone I had the privilege of working with- in order to protect his identity, we will call him John. John was a very lively man that you'd want to work with or hang with off duty. He is also a large man who had a lot of medical issues. He suffered from PTSD and it didn't help that he had financial troubles too. All of this made for a very stressful life. I first met John during my second year in the police department. It was in traffic court- we were both there because of tickets we wrote for people speeding and various other traffic violations. As we were waiting in the hallway for our turn to testify, we started talking about a wide variety of topics, from our jobs to our personal lives. He was a very interesting conversationalist, and I immediately made a connection with him. We became friends from that moment on.

A year later, a spot opened up in the DWI task force unit and I applied for it, wanting to try something different than patrol. It was also a way to build my resume and further my career. John was already on the task force squad for traffic. He shot the laser and radar on freeways, stopping people for speeding violations, in hopes of running across a DWI suspect. I reached out to him to let him know I was waiting for my interview for the unit. He went over all of the stuff they would question me about and gave me more tips to help with the interview.

I sat down with three sergeants during the interview and they went through my files and my disciplinary history and also my awards and accommodations. They started firing questions at me, one after the other, about DWI procedures and issues pertaining to the department in the unit. After about 30 minutes of tough questioning, I was told they would contact me after all 20 applicants have been interviewed. I stood up, shook their hands, and walked out of there feeling very confident about the process so far.

Later that day, John called me to say that they liked me,, and that I did well on the scenario questions. Two days passed and no one reached out to me. I was feeling like shit, especially since I knew I did a great job. I called my old man, who at the time was a sergeant assigned to the motorcycle unit (SOLO), and told him that I probably did not get the job. My Dad told me to not worry about it, and that another spot would open up. He knew there were others on the force that were just as qualified as me and I was still considered a rookie with just a few years on. He advised me to keep an eye out for the next chance to reapply for another interview.

As soon as I hung up the phone with him, my phone rang and it was the sergeant I interviewed with. He told me I made the cut and that I would start the very next day. I thanked him for this opportunity and hung up feeling excited. I got a call from my old man saying how happy he was to hear the news- it turns out he already knew before and didn't tell me. He said that now I would be working in the traffic division and this meant that we could work overtime together. I was glad I would be working with him sometimes since we didn't see each other very often with our schedules.

After working with John for a few months, I noticed that he had to take five or six pills every couple of hours for different health reasons. He was definitely a workaholic and he also loved junk food. He was by far the nicest and most fun person I knew, which is why I kept trying to get him to eat healthy. He was a huge man, standing about 5'11 and weighing well over 350 pounds. He wasn't interested in giving up junk food and he seemed very happy with his lifestyle. He also had his own cot set up in our office so that he could take naps when he was between or before court appearances. It seemed like he never went to his home. We were a tag-team on traffic stops along with other officers in the unit. He would shoot a laser, I would pull the cars over, and then we would switch roles.

All in all, during the time that I worked with him and before I fell into my own dark hole, he seemed to manage his own PTSD quite well. Perhaps the regimen of his lifestyle helped him a lot. Having deep introspection, taking responsibility, and being pragmatic in finding the best way to manage the effects of PTSD is always necessary if one is to be finally free from its enslavement.

Ice Patch

It was 5:00 a.m. one morning and my shift was almost over. I was still assigned to the DWI task force and was heading back to the station from the southeastern area of Houston. It was freezing outside and the streets were covered with icy patches, haphazardly placed all over the road. The freeway was unkind to the inexperienced driver, so I was driving slowly to keep the appropriate pace for the cars around me. As I was heading downtown, I approached a large elevated section of the Gulf freeway, and as I felt my tires sliding, I quickly put on the brakes and tapped them to prevent skidding. I could see a stranded vehicle at the bottom of the hill positioned in the middle of the freeway and taking up two lanes. It was sitting sideways in the middle of the main lanes. I started moving slowly toward the vehicle with my emergency lights on so other drivers who are headed our way could see us early enough. I inched my way to the vehicle and noticed that there was an elderly woman sitting in the driver's seat. She had that look of fear on her face like she was stuck and lost.

As a police officer, I have seen that look on so many people. She said that she lost control on the ice, slid and hit the median, pushing her out into the middle of the freeway. I asked her if she was hurt and she said she was not. When I reached in to get her out of her car, I could see through her passenger side window that a vehicle was losing control at the top of the hill and heading our way. I quickly shoved her back into the car and buckled her seat belt to protect her, just in case she got hit. I figured she would be safer buckled in than outside the vehicle in the main lanes. I ran toward the vehicle coming at us, waving my flashlight to get the attention of the driver. One moment I was running, and the next minute I slipped on an icy patch and fell, hitting my head on the ice. I looked up to see another car hit the median, spin out of control, and head toward me at an uncontrollable speed. In a split second, I tucked my head into my chest and prayed it would miss me, since I didn't have enough time to move. I could hear and feel the gust of wind from that car as it sped past my head, barely missing me and the car with the elderly woman. I quickly got up and noticed that there were four more cars losing control in the same spot and all four of them started hitting the medians, heading right toward us. I ran up the hill, flashing lights at them to get their attention. Just then, a tall black gentleman in work overalls who pulled over on the side of the freeway after seeing what just happened got out of his vehicle, wanting to help me.

He yelled out to me, "What can I do to help?"

I yelled back to him, "Nothing! Get back in your vehicle until everything is under control!"

I kept running up the hill. After getting on the radio, trying to get help, I had a few local wrecker drivers help close down the freeway. They saved my life and the lives of the people in the now eight wrecked vehicles on the freeway. I ran from car to car to see who had the most severe injuries and found a military man in his uniform who had a huge laceration in his leg. I tore a shirt he had in his car and quickly tied it on him to slow the bleeding. By then I had a few officers show up and start helping all the wounded around us. After gathering everyone's information, the wrecker driver yelled out to me that there was a body on the feeder road directly under the elevated section where we were. I rushed to the edge, looked down, and saw that it was the man I yelled at earlier to get back in his car. He had his mind set so hard on helping the wounded that he ignored me and kept checking on vehicles, when a vehicle spun out of control and hit him – sending him over the ledge and face first into the concrete sidewalk that was approximately 50 feet below, crushing his head. He died instantly from the impact. This man died helping people.

In the 13 years that I've been a police officer, I have personally seen humanity at its finest and at its worst. That morning I saw a man on his way to work who was pulled into a lose-lose situation, yet fought to help save lives. I will always see his face and his willingness to help his brothers and sisters, no matter the circumstance. This is why we do this job. We know there are people out there like that man.

As I made it back to the old lady in the first vehicle, I observed her hands clenched to the steering wheel and her face was in shock. Other than that, she and her vehicle were in one piece, untouched. While I was walking toward her, I remember thinking to myself, "How the hell did this just happen? How did this lady not even get a scratch on her vehicle after all this craziness that just happened? As I approached her driver's side door and opened it, I began with, "Ma'am," and before I could finish, she jumped into my arms hugging me telling me that I was her guardian angel and that I saved her life. I let her hug me and told her everything was okay now.

We rarely get told we do a good job and to be honest, I am not that fond of "Attaboys," but when it comes from a person who really means every word, a person who truly believes you saved them, it is a feeling no one can explain. I live for those feelings in this job.

After we cleared off the freeway and the accident division helped me gather everyone's information, I heard that one of the officers in my unit was rushing to my scene to help me when I first yelled on the mic for help, and crashed on the way. He rode up into a median after spinning out on some ice; he had a cut on his head as a result of the wreckage and suffered from a broken leg. Later I found out that when I got on the mic, my colleagues could hear the sound of cars crashing in the background and it sounded pretty intense.

The truth, however, is that no matter how intense a situation is or how dangerous a situation is, you have brothers and sisters racing to you, ready to die for you to help. This is our brotherhood. This is why we are stronger than regular friendships. We are family. And like the others, I'll be there for my family no matter what the situation is. We stick by each other because we are all we have on the streets. I absolutely love this job and the people in it.

"There was a time where I cried every day. It would be a wave of emotion that just came over me. My friends are dead. And if that doesn't bother you, then you are made of something different than I am."

~ Chief Warrant Officer Mike Durant (POW during Desert Storm)

Chapter 7:
The Mental Toll on the Officer

The toll that our work takes on us has pushed quite a number of good officers into ending their own lives. When the mental struggles of officers are brought to the forefront, all we can do is reach out to them and let them know we are here for anything they need. However, this can be difficult because in your mind you don't want to seem too aggressive and risk crossing a boundary.

Losing a friend

Around the time that I was facing my own self-doubts after an unfortunate event, disturbing and shocking news filtered in to add salt to injury.

I was placed in our Property Division on a temporary assignment to get me out of the public's eye because the media was dragging my name through the mud over a shooting of a man who was later found out to be mentally ill (this story will not be in this book). At first, I was pissed off because I still wanted to "run and gun" and I missed the excitement that was easily found working the streets. After a while, my body adjusted to the hours and I noticed I was sleeping a lot better for some reason. During this time, I was unable to work extra jobs because of the active investigation, which meant I couldn't keep myself busy by working gigs outside the department.

One day while I was at the office working, I started getting text messages back to back from a number of officers about a gunshot coming from the parking garage across the street at the Central Police Station. As I was trying to see what was going on, I saw ambulances rushing into the station's garage, and officers running over to the area. After calling a friend of mine who worked at the station, I learned that John had taken his own life. He was found sitting slumped behind the wheel of his patrol car with a bullet hole in his head. I couldn't believe it. I called more people and his name kept coming up and when it was finally confirmed, my heart dropped. I was devastated. He couldn't find a way out.

I started blaming myself. I thought that if I had reached out to him more often it might have made a difference. I was driving myself crazy, questioning every thought that came into my mind and picking it apart until it was nothing but shreds. Then the next, "what if..." and the other questions after that followed. It was driving me crazy.

John is gone. It was just hard to see anything straight during that period of time in my life with this added to everything else I was going through.

Post-traumatic Stress Disorder (PTSD) is more common than you think. People who have it will act like everything is always okay and downplay the severity of it. The way to spot people who have PTSD is to look at how they act and also the way they speak. Many of you may have encountered people struggling with PTSD, but it can be hard to know exactly how to deal with them or help them.

People can get PTSD from anything traumatic that may have happened in their lives. For instance, I know people who got it from horrific car accidents where someone lost a life or they almost lost their own. PTSD is most commonly diagnosed in those in the military, combat or non-combat. Either way, the experiences that they faced affected them to the point where it altered their train of thought, sleep patterns, awareness, the way they looked, and also their health. Stress can cause so many health issues within the body and if it is ignored long enough, it could cause serious emotional and even physical pain for the individual and others who live around them.

With family

PTSD affects a person's immediate family, close friends, and anyone who comes into contact with that person. When you think that someone is suffering from this, please pull him or her aside and ask if everything is okay, and if there is anything you can do to help. You should do it in such a way that it doesn't cause a scene and without anyone else knowing. I say this because some people are ashamed of having PTSD and don't want anybody else knowing. There are many reasons for this. One may be because they don't want people at their work to worry about them, or they don't want people feeling sorry for them, or they may just not want the attention that comes along with having it. If that person is unwilling to speak about it, don't pressure them – just make sure you let them know that you are there if they need you. If it gets to the point where it's obvious something serious is wrong with that person, notify somebody else about this, whether it be their family or their immediate supervisors. You never know what people are thinking and you never know how extreme it can really get without help.

Chapter 8:
Living With PTSD

Overwhelming Guilt

After the horrific incident of taking a man's life, I experienced a lot of emotions all at once. These thoughts, along with the daydreams and nightmares that came along with it, affected my life in many ways. The effects from this incident were both positive and negative, and in some ways changed my life permanently. This life experience caused me to deal with the guilt and the after-thoughts of killing a man in the line of duty.

Growing up in the church, killing someone was always the number one sin someone could do that would ensure a one-way trip down south when our time is up on earth. After numerous confession sessions on my own in the privacy of my bedside, I still feel as if the guilt is with me. Everyone in my family and people close to me say I should go to church and confess to the preacher so that I can feel better about my situation. The problem is that I didn't feel as if I deserve to even set foot in a church after the incident happened.

This incident happened on a late fall night in October at

an apartment complex in the East End of Houston. I was on a traffic stop conducting a field sobriety test on a young male who was driving on the Gulf Freeway and was unable to stay in one lane. But he passed all the tests given to him, and I learned he was just fatigued from long shifts at work so I let him go home.

My colleague met up with me and while talking to him I heard an assault with a deadly weapon call drop on his car radio, not even 200 yards away from our location.

My colleague and I both took the call and started heading over. As we pulled in, I could see a man stabbing a woman on the balcony that was facing the street. We jumped out of our patrol cars and pushed through the crowd that had gathered around and were throwing objects at the man trying to get him to stop. As I arrived at the top of the staircase, my colleague was yelling verbal commands to him to drop the knife which was an 8 ½ inch kitchen knife, tearing into the flesh with every thrust he took. I noticed that his focus was on an old man who was being a Good Samaritan that was only trying to help the woman. I saw the suspect stab the old man two times in the stomach and was going for a third raising the knife over his head.

Lifesaving award

Unable to have time to fully process in my mind what was going on, I raised my duty weapon and shot the out-of-control man two times in the arm. Since he was not squared up with me, I could not aim at his chest. I think after watching the movies and seeing people fly back after getting shot, it made me believe I had missed him because he did not stop immediately. It seemed as if I made the man even angrier because then he looked directly at me with a blank stare and raised the knife and took two steps toward my colleague. Since my colleague still has his gun in his holster, I shot for the third time, hitting the man in the neck and causing him to instantly drop to the ground, lifeless.

I immediately rushed over to him and kicked the large

knife away from his body, which was now covered in blood. I then went to the old man who was trying to get up, but was slipping on his own blood and falling back down. After calming him down, I had him lay on his side and heard him asking me for help. The strikes from the knife had already done damage and his insides were falling out with every breath he was gasping for. He died soon after, before the medics could arrive.

I then went to the woman who was stabbed when we first arrived at the location. She was crying and unable to speak. Her face was pale from the amount of blood that she had lost from her wounds. I immediately observed a cluster of deep stab wounds on her back and right shoulder. Her body was shooting out blood, causing a huge puddle on the ground around her. I tried getting information from her before the ambulance arrived, but she couldn't speak due to the shock her body was in. This young lady was going in and out of consciousness as I kept slapping her in her face to keep her awake.

The Houston Fire Department arrived and told me a number of times to move away and let them take over. My adrenaline and nerves were going all at once and I had "tunnel vision," in a zone where everything but the female pouring blood from her body was blocked out of my mind. By the time I was pulled off of her she had a t-shirt around her wounds which slowed the loss of blood.

After HFD (Houston Fire Department) carried her off the balcony, I was in shock looking at the aftermath that the crazed man left behind. It was bloodier than anything I have seen.

I looked down at my feet and I noticed that my boots were covered in the blood of both the old man and the young woman. The white walls and the ceiling of the balcony walkway were also sprayed red.

As I looked down at myself I noticed my right hand, which I used to pull the trigger with, would not stop shaking. Embarrassed as to what my colleagues would say, I quickly shoved my hand in my pants pocket. I find it weird that in the middle of this craziness my "macho" side still worried about looking weak in the eyes of the people who depend on me to back them up or handle situations on the street.

"What's wrong with me?" I said to myself quietly walking to the patrol car. I never thought I would have to end someone's life.

To make matters worse, during the walk through of the scene with the Brass and IA we hear car tires screeching to a stop. As we looked out onto the side street near the apartment complex, a drunk driver almost hit a patrol car where my DWI unit had set up for support. The officers quickly pulled the intoxicated man out of the driver's seat and placed him under arrest after giving him some tests. I remember thinking about how insane that night had been.

Afterwards I asked myself, "Why me? Why was he doing something so crazy?" I wondered what he was thinking. A million questions were racing through my head all at once. The whole time I was in the Homicide Division and writing the report, my mind was somewhere else. Before I knew it, I was in the shower in my apartment and in my mind the water running down my body turned into blood. "Am I going crazy?" I asked myself as tears ran down my face. I couldn't remember the last time I cried.

I remember how quickly I took a life, with three pulls of my index finger. This was the first time I took a life – and the fact that it happened in a crazy situation worsened the feeling. From then on, my thoughts about life changed so much.

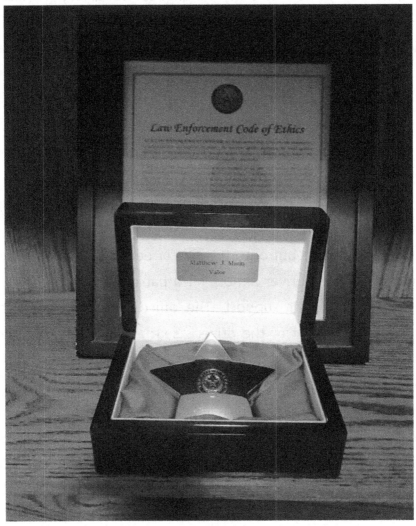

Award of Valor

That incident showed me that I had it inside me to do

my job and take a life in order to save a life. It showed me how my father and mother played a big role as I was growing up, by helping me through all the hard times that life threw my way.

Dealing with the guilt of killing a man and not being able to save another one is still with me, but I am taking steps to understand this incident and why it happened. The nightmares and questions still pop up in my head here and there, but it became more controlled later when I got therapy. The awards I received for this incident is a constant reminder that what I did was appreciated by the State of Texas and the city of Houston. I love my job and have no regrets. I am confident in my skills because I have been trained by the very best in Houston. Often, I believe that these types of life-changing events do not happen by accident. Everything happens for a reason. I felt changed by three quick pulls of the trigger.

After the Shooting

The morning after my shooting and with hardly any sleep the night before, I was told I had to see a counselor and talk about my feelings. This had never happened to me before: killing a man or seeing a shrink. I can remember the awkwardness I felt because I honestly didn't even understand my own feelings about the entire situation. I just remember that a lot of questions kept swirling around in my head. I also felt a lot of guilt for not being able to get there in time to save the older gentleman who was stabbed and lost his life.

While I was sitting on the couch in the counselor's office, I wondered, "What does she want from me?" But there I sat, looking at this middle-aged woman who I met before in my academy class. She taught us for a day about the importance of counseling in our line of work. Now that I was finally there in that hot seat, I had trouble focusing on her words. Tons of thoughts were racing through my head while she spoke to me. I was there, but wasn't there mindfully at all. I stared into space while the entire scene played back like a recording set on replay. Each time I went over the scene, I remembered more and more about that night, including the smallest details and the quick actions that took place.

I snapped out of it when she repeated my name a few times and I apologized for not paying attention. She offered comfort by telling me not to apologize. She said that what I was going through was normal. I also remember thinking " you have no idea what I'm going through."

She stopped talking long enough to give me a notepad and told me to list all of the highly stressful situations that have happened in my life up until now. She felt it was a good place for us to start. She wanted to get an idea of my feelings, and what she was dealing with. She stepped out of the room for a few minutes and I started listing them, including events that occurred in my childhood and military days. When she came back into the room, I already had over ten incidents written down. She stopped me and read the list to herself. She then said that she was very concerned about me having been through all this stuff at an early age and that she wanted me to get on a program with her to help me through whatever I was feeling about these incidents and especially the one that just happened. I told her that I would do whatever she thought would help me, and that I wanted to get back on the streets as soon as possible.

What I didn't tell her was that the reason I wanted to go back on the streets to patrol was to get my mind off of the shooting. I was tired of the chatter, the voice that just wouldn't set me free. She stated that department policy states that I had to take off three days after the shooting and then get evaluated to go back.

After my session, I remember driving home and just zoning out, thinking of different scenarios of how the outcome would have been different two nights before. I remember thinking about the older man who died and his face looking up at me as life left his body, and I can remember the feeling I had, knowing I couldn't do anything at all to save him. I am definitely not the crying type, but in my Hummer on the way home, I started crying uncontrollably over this old man and remembering his family there at the scene, looking at me and expecting me to help him and save his life. I had to pull over at a gas station to get my shit together. That brave man, that hero, didn't deserve to die that way. The feeling of worthlessness came over me again reminding me of my failure.

When I arrived at my apartment, I went straight to my bedroom, threw myself on my bed and just laid there in silence for hours. Wide awake and zoned out, embroiled in my thoughts, I could not attend to my phone even though it was going off the hook from family and friends calling to check on me. I ignored all of it and just laid there. This was definitely the lowest I had ever been in my entire life. I can remember that at one point late in the night I went for the whiskey I had saved for special occasions. Well, this wasn't the special occasion I had in mind.

But there I was, on the couch with tears in my eyes: my gun in one hand and a glass of whiskey in the other staring into a blank TV screen that was turned off. After an unknown amount of time sitting there in stupor, I snapped out of it and put the gun down, having no idea at all why I had the gun in my hand. I needed help and I knew it would only get worse if I didn't get it.

I hoped at that point that counseling would work. It didn't work out immediately as I spiraled downward a few years later. Things only came back to normal when I was ready to take the bull by the horns and move on.

Returning to Work

Two days after I returned to work from the shooting, the DWI (Driving While Intoxicated) unit had a meeting with the entire chain of command present at headquarters. They were going over updates and talking about getting new equipment. During the five days that I was off, I did not sleep well. I had been sleeping for about 30 minutes at a time off and on since the shooting. As we met up at the main police building downtown I remember riding up the elevator alone, staring at the ceiling and leaning up against the wall. I knew I wasn't ready to come back yet. I had to make it through this meeting so I could get back home because at least there I would be away from people.

I stepped off the elevator and saw my unit and supervisors hanging around outside of the conference room, socializing before the meeting. I walked past everyone, avoiding any eye contact, and made my way into the conference room where I took a seat and waited for it to start. After about five minutes of waiting, people started to trickle in, little by little, and took their seats. I remember sitting there in a daze, with my mind not concerned about the meeting at all. I was fixated on a random spot on the floor in front of me. The meeting started and all I heard was mumbling from a distance while one of our supervisors was speaking.

When I snapped out of my daydream, I found my sergeant tapping me on my shoulder and asking if I was okay. I looked around the room and all eyes were on me, their faces showing genuine concern. The sergeant and lieutenant asked me to step out into the hallway, so nervously I did. When we got outside of the conference room I was scared they were going to send me back to the psychologist for observation and take away my badge.

As the other supervisors came outside to see how I was doing, my sergeant asked me if I was okay, and I responded, "Yes sir." Knowing my old man was an officer, he said that he wanted me to go home and spend a few days with my Dad to calm myself down, and then come back when I was ready.

In my head, I was incredibly angry because working was the only thing that took my mind off of the incident. However, I agreed with him and the other supervisors showed me nothing but support by saying things like, "You did a great job out there," and "We got your back on this and if you need anything, let us know." I shook their hands and walked back into the elevator. I felt ashamed and weak for letting the experience control me in public. I was embarrassed. This was a new low for me.

I was not able to sleep very much at all, so I would pick up as many extra shifts as I could and on the days I could not work, I would go to the clubs. The clubs were literally five minutes away from where I lived so I would have some drinks, smoke a cigar, and just try to relax by myself as loud music played while I was deep in thought. During this time also, I formed many relationships that I later regretted. I enjoyed them at the time because they never got jealous or got dramatic over things I considered trivial because their emotions and actions were mostly independent of mine, never asking for anything in return. I made it clear that I did not want a serious relationship because I just got out of one. They all understood, and comically, they all knew about each other. This lasted until 2011.

That was one of my coping mechanisms but it was also quite hazardous. I still dealt with constant visions and the guilt caused a number of incidents I went through in life as well. Sometimes I would get up in the middle of the night and walk around the perimeter of my house and apartments with my gun on me because I heard weird noises while I slept. Drinking became an everyday thing. I did it to temporarily drown out the vivid motion picture replaying over and over in my head.

When I wasn't drinking, I was picking up any and every extra shift at work to keep my mind busy. Our department had a 16-hour limit on our work days so officers don't get too tired and work two or three days straight without any time off. I used to max out this limit practically every day. I thought that if I stayed busy it wouldn't give my mind the opportunity to have flashbacks or dreams. But working too many hours took its toll on me and led to unexpected dozing off which sometimes made me late to appointments, meetings, courts and roll calls. It also caused some friction with my supervisors at work because of the issues I listed.

On the downside, all these hours of work would make me be super tired on my time off and would just drown myself in alcohol whenever I wasn't working, killing every relationship I had. I would go to clubs constantly and bring home women on a regular basis. Rock bottom hurts, especially when you add guilt and alcohol to the mix. It was during this time that I would wake up drenched in sweat, or screaming from a fit, or even swinging wildly in the air. I dated a lady around this time and I succeeded in scaring her enough that she left me. She said I woke up swinging and accidentally pushed her off the bed in the process. This was all before I sought a treatment that worked.

I remember one time my colleagues wanted to go out and bar around the area we used to patrol. When I got there to meet up with them I remember immediately asking myself why the hell I came. As I walked into the small cantina on the east end of Houston, I saw about six of the guys I worked with waving at me to come sit down at their table. As I made my way over to them I was approached by a waitress who took my whiskey order and left to get it for me. I can remember the guys complimenting me on what I did; they said it like it was a cool thing. I absolutely hated it.

When I first got on the department, I had absolutely zero interest in using my firearm. As a matter of fact, I never practiced with it, other than in our annual qualifier we had to accomplish to keep our jobs. For not practicing at all, I still always shot above average so qualifying never worried me. My father spent a ton of time with me training me to shoot when I was growing up. But the officers in the bar started talking about all these new guns they bought and how they go and train with them on their off days and debating why and how they would shoot a criminal if it was absolutely necessary. I have learned that in this line of work, the loud mouth cops are usually the ones who buckle under pressure and the quieter ones are the ones who usually do what needs to be done. Not all the time, but at least for the most part.

As time went on, hearing stupid story after stupid story about the calls they had on duty and how badass they thought they were, I was losing my temper. I came out here to relax, not talk about work or criminals. I got up and walked out of the bar and went straight to a club where some of the girls I messed around with were. One of them who worked at the club took off and came home with me after seeing how distraught I was.

I have no idea why, but for some weird reason, I found that these girls were my outlet. None of them expected anything from me at all, nor did they hound me. I guess in my head I was using them as a stress reliever. One of the clubs was literally right around the corner from my apartment and is where I spent many nights drinking these thoughts and visions away. On my days off I would hate to fall asleep because of the dreams I was having. Clubs were definitely an attraction for me. Afterwards, I would go right around the corner to my apartment and pass out, usually waking up to a random girl who came home with me after I sweet talked them in the clubs. I knew this was not the life I wanted to live, but at the time it seemed like the best thing for me to do to occupy my time and get affection from women without all the trouble of having a girlfriend.

My colleagues would ask me why I left early sometimes and why I didn't go out with them very much and I just said it wasn't my thing and that I preferred being by myself, which in a way was the truth. I was going through so much emotionally and mentally at the time that I didn't want to have anyone around. Another reason why I separated myself from people a lot was because of my increasing bad temper. Everything seemed to aggravate me during this period. I found it interesting that when I was on duty dealing with the public and domestic disturbances and people acting out, it didn't affect me, but when I was off duty and dealing with people in my personal life, I would get mad very quickly and show my impatience.

"We have come too far to turn back, we owe ourselves to live again. Yet, we owe it to our fallen comrades. Let us live life for them in their honor."

~ The Voice
(Road to recovery video) YouTube

Chapter 9:
Educating and Healing Yourself

I believe that as a society, we don't discuss the mental health of police officers enough. The fact that officers have to unconsciously pile their struggles onto the ones they encounter daily on calls should get them to be more motivated to seek help. After I suffered bouts of traumatic episodes for years, I finally sought help.

For me, dealing with the guilt of not being able to save a life but being able to end it in just a split moment broke me for some time. My department finally got me to attend a 4-day LEMIT seminar, and it changed my life. I was there with 12 other officers from all around Texas where we stayed together on campus at the Sam Houston State facility.

Hanging out with friends and family

In this program, we went through EMDR (Eye Movement Desensitization and Reprocessing), and then after, we engaged in 60 - 90 minute sessions where you would talk about your traumatic event with your therapist, and how it has affected your life. The next stage was to write in detail about what happened at the traumatic event. This procedure helped me to figure out new ways to live with my trauma.

Other things were also useful for my recovery - my dog, visiting with Veterans of Foreign Wars (VFW), and going to a shooting range to relieve some stress all helped with my therapy.

Eye Opener

One major incident in my life that helped me realize isolating myself wasn't the way to live was when I experienced the loss of a loved one that was very close to me.

My aunt Gloria was a beautiful mother of two who was always taking care of her family, myself included. Growing up, she would babysit me and my siblings pretty regularly. She was a loving woman who would do anything for us, even though I'm pretty sure we were a headache —when I say we, I mean her son and I. My cousin was a few years older than I was and we would sneak out and go to parties when I stayed over-it would drive my aunt crazy. Even though we never listened, she always showed me love, and I never questioned her love for me. Over the years, I learned that my aunt was suffering from a rare disease called Scleroderma, which is an autoimmune disease of the tissue caused by increased production of the protein collagen in the body tissues. Unfortunately, there is no cure for this disease. Her primary symptoms were hardening and tightening of the skin and tissue.

After decades of fighting this disease, my aunt finally couldn't take it anymore and was taken to the hospital where she was made comfortable until the time came where she felt it was ok to go. In a way, I was happy for her because not a lot of people have any say so in how and when they pass away, but with her, she was able to have the entire family stay with her at the hospital and was able to speak to each of us separately.

As I waited to speak to her, I didn't know what I was going

to say to her. What do you say to someone who is about to die, especially someone that you love and care for? As my Mom waved me in from the hallway where I was waiting, sitting on the ground against the wall, I walked in and there she was lying in bed connected to machines. Immediately, I started crying inside, but I tried not to let her see me because I didn't want that to be her last image of me. I walked up to her bed and told her I loved her. She looked at me and told me that she was proud of me and that our family should always come first, that she knew I had gone through things and that I needed to deal with them and be there for the family. This hit me like a brick wall- my heart dropped with the weight of knowing that I isolated myself a lot so that they wouldn't see how the trauma I endured made me. She went on to tell me that the only thing that helps us through tough times is family. After we were done speaking, I kissed her on her forehead and told her I loved her. I then walked out so that the next person to come in and speak to her. Sitting in the hallway and staying overnight at the hospital with the whole family there, I realized that I lost a lot of time with her and the rest of my family by being selfish and trying to stay away for the fear of them not accepting me.

The time came to where my aunt was ready to turn off the machines and let herself drift away into the Heavens. The immediate family went in and shut the door, we all gathered around the bedside, talking and laughing with each other while listening to her playlist of favorites which included Michael Jackson, The Eagles and a few others. This is definitely the way I would wish to die when it is my time, surrounded by the people I love the most. Looking back at it, this made me proud to be a part of a family that is so close and that is there for each other. You gain knowledge through other people's suffering and your own as well- and after you get through it, your view of life is different.

Relieving stress

"The second highest diagnosis behind PTSD is depression, and if left untreated, people turn to substance abuse. So, we really need to intervene as soon as we can."

~Kathleen M. Chard, PhD (Director of the Trauma Recovery Center for the VA)

Chapter 10:
How to Help Someone Spot Symptoms of PTSD

By now, you understand how deeply distressing a trauma can be, particularly because it overwhelms your ability to cope with routine life situations When someone struggles with PTSD, he/she experiences that agony, even after that traumatizing event has passed, because the person cannot let go of the impact that episode left on his/her body, mind, and soul.

While there is nothing abnormal about going through PTSD and it most definitely is not something we should treat as taboo, it is also important to deal with it effectively and as soon as one identifies it. It is important to look for the different signs and symptoms of PTSD so you can help the affected person promptly and he or she can return to a happy, balanced life as soon as possible.

The problem with the signs of PTSD is that oftentimes they do not occur right away. While some people exhibit those symptoms soon after going through a trauma, others may take some time to become visible on the surface. Also, oftentimes, the signs somehow seem disconnected to the actual event and manifest themselves in ways that seem completely unrelated to the main distressing episode. With that being said, if you pay attention to some cues and the general behavior of the person you suspect is struggling with PTSD, you can spot the problem on time.

Our loved ones need our support and help, especially during difficult times. You may have seen how everyone jumps in to celebrate your achievements with you. However, hardly any of those people are there for you when you are aching from within. Sadly, this is how our society functions. However, it is up to you to make that positive difference in society that it so desperately needs.

Making that difference isn't difficult. You just need to nurture an empathetic heart that can feel the pain and plight of others. Teach yourself to imagine yourself in your loved one's shoes. Pay attention to their behavior and problems, and then help them identify and gradually work towards overcoming the issue or problem for good.

Your loved ones may not say it to you out loud, but everyone who goes through suffering, including the aching brought upon by PTSD, wants someone who can identify their grief and help them manage it for good. That means your best friend who has just returned after an especially challenging tour, your partner in the police department, or your aunt who just lost her young son, covertly wishes to have someone who is not afraid to reach out and offer help.

Because you are a kind, loving soul, take it upon yourself to help your loved one understand and spot the signs of PTSD in their demeanor. This is a tricky job as you have to do it very carefully, making sure that the person you are trying to help does not feel offended.

As is usually the case, people who have PTSD often become very rigid to any suggestions or opinions, particularly those related to personal improvement. Deep down, the person knows that he/she is struggling with some problem (often not clear exactly what though), but finds it hard to come to terms with accepting it. Accepting an issue especially related to mental health is never easy, primarily because for a long time, mental health has held a stigma in our society.

Slowly help your loved one understand that struggling with mental health issues is not taboo at all and it's not something to shy away from accepting. It is just an ailment like a common cold or fever- it needs time, attention, and proper treatment. The primary step of curbing the issue is to identify it.

You can use the following signs and symptoms of PTSD to spot in your loved ones in need of your immediate help.

Intense Rage

Intense and volatile anger is one of the first signs of PTSD you should aim to notice. Does the person have an extremely "short fuse" these days? Does he or she lose their temper on trivial matters? Has your brother/sister in the police or military started getting road-rage the instant someone cuts into their driving lane? Does your partner in the police department become irritable and aggressive often? Do you feel that the rage is often quite extreme, especially in situations that don't call for anger?

If you observe these issues in a loved one, it is very likely that he or she is struggling with PTSD and is either unable to identify it or maybe knows it but cannot accept it alone. The speed at which someone reacts to an event with anger is one of the crucial and most important symptoms of PTSD. Different routine life situations and experiences can trigger the pain the person once went through or may stir up grief that the person wasn't originally aware of during the actual trauma. That can create an urge to fight back the pain with anger. Unfortunately, this only worsens the problem.

Pay attention to your loved one's behavior in everyday life and look for any signs of intense, unexplainable, and irrational anger. Every time you see your loved one behave irrationally or act angrily to petty issues, take note of that.

Do not instantly and directly bring up that issue with your loved one. You need to observe you're loved one for some time very cautiously and secretly until you are sure that the person truly has PTSD.

Hypervigilance

A traumatizing event tends to make one very alert and edgy. A person with PTSD is likely to be very alert all the time and may become very edgy and oversensitive in life's normal situations.

That happens because the actual trauma triggered the fight or flight mechanism, and the person is now unable to turn it off. He or she is still in that survival mode governed by a rush of adrenaline and cortisol that keeps him or her on edge and ready to fight, flee or freeze in an upsetting and shocking situation.

Has your sister, who served as a nurse in the army, started becoming jumpy around certain people or topics? Does your police partner flinch in terror every time someone pats him on the back? Does your brother instantly jump nervously each time he senses someone is at the door? If you do find a loved one displaying extreme hyper-vigilance in situations that do not need that kind of alertness, he or she is likely battling a trauma.

Emptiness and Numbness

Most people struggling with PTSD develop a coping mechanism of completely switching off from a situation. It is like that person is not even in the room; he or she goes completely numb. While this may not seem normal to you, it is how the person copes with the pain he or she is fighting inside of them For your loved one, the trauma he or she went through some time back still feels live and real. It is constantly playing in their head, and every time that pain grows more intense, the more they switch themselves off so that they can stop feeling that ache at least for a small window of time.

Those going through PTSD from trauma frequently experience intense flashbacks of that traumatic episode. Scenes from that horrific circumstance start to play in their head unconsciously, and before they realize it, they feel flooded with that pain and misery all over again.

Has your loved one suddenly started losing interest in what's going on around them? Has he or she started looking lost, and not paying attention to anything you or other people say to them? If that's the case, perhaps a disturbing memory has engulfed your loved one. Look for this sign in your loved one to help confirm if they are facing symptoms of PTSD.

Difficulties Sleeping

Has your partner who recently returned home after a tour started waking up in the middle of the night, screaming in pain or agony? Does your cop friend often tell you of how they have been feeling restless for nights and hasn't had a good night's sleep in weeks?

It can be very difficult for those going through PTSD to sleep well at night. While nighttime is a peaceful time for many, for those struggling with PTSD it's not as calming. Since everything around them is quiet, such people find it easy to slip back into their painful memories.

It's likely that your loved one keeps having flashbacks throughout the night, preventing them from sleeping well. Even if they do, they end up waking up from one nightmare or another. Oftentimes nightmares are attempts by the unconscious mind to try to fix the original trauma.

It is easier to spot sleeping difficulties and occurrences of nightmares in the person you are trying to help, particularly if you share the same roof. However, for people that don't live with you but that you suspect may be going through PTSD, get into the habit of inquiring after their sleep patterns in covert ways. You can casually slip in statements about how you have been sleeping well regularly and how that has improved your wellbeing. You can also informally ask the person how he or she slept at night.

If your relationship with that person allows it, or if you feel a bit bold, you can even tell the person how the eye bags under their eyes concern you. Or even how they look too sleepy and tired during the day — as if they did not sleep well. You can then use that as a way to drive the conversation towards learning more about their sleep patterns.

Also, constantly observe your loved ones for any signs of lethargy, lack of focus, irritability, exhaustion, and loss of interest. If you see your friend dozing off while talking to you, or your partner feeling incredibly lethargic even though they told you they slept well, it is likely they aren't sleeping well and may be experiencing interruptions in their sleep at night.

However, lack of sleep and insomnia can be due to many other problems as well, which is why you need to look out for other signs of PTSD in your loved ones.

Withdrawing from Certain Activities or Avoiding Certain People/ Places

For those going through PTSD, numerous things can serve as triggers. Your loved one may become jittery upon seeing your burly neighbor because that may remind him of a person he encountered in a police operation. Your veteran sister who almost died clearing a building at night may not feel comfortable going into dark, closed spaces anymore.

Your loved ones may not directly tell you of what happens to them in certain places or with certain people, or when engaging in certain activities. However, the chances are high that these factors remind them of the traumatic event. They likely stir up thoughts, feelings, and emotions that perturb them for hours and even days at times. If you notice that a certain loved one has started withdrawing from social situations, losing interest in activities they found enjoyable before a traumatic event, or disengaging with certain people, your loved one may be having a hard time with PTSD.

Suffer from Self-Blame and Self-Guilt

In most instances, when someone survives a tough situation or a life-threatening experience while another person in the scenario dies, the survivor goes through 'survivor's guilt,' a feeling of self-guilt that makes the person feel bad for surviving the trauma.

Pay attention to how your loved one speaks about that traumatic episode and observe their speech. Does the person constantly talk about how bad he or she feels for living while someone else lost their life? About how they should have died instead of the other person? If you notice any of this, it should be a clear sign that the person is going through feelings of self-blame and needs your help to heal and get on the road to recovery.

Severe Mood Swings

Besides the signs of PTSD discussed above, look for occurrences of severe mood swings in the loved one you are trying to help. If your friend seems perfectly fine one minute but loses their cool in another instant, that's a sign that something may not be right with your friend. Maybe, they wander off in thought to that painful memory of how they were nearly shot, or of another crime scene that they experienced.

Mood swings may or may not accompany bouts of volatile anger. Sometimes, a mood swing may just make your loved one lose interest in something, become agitated for no reason, or excuse themselves from a situation so that they can go into isolation. That is why you need to observe different aspects of a mood swing and not just intense rage.

Endeavor to notice these signs in your loved one by observing him or her covertly for 7 to 10 days. If the person or loved one in question checks off 3 to 5 of these signs, including intense anger, withdrawing from certain activities, insomnia, and feeling numb, every indicator is that person is going through PTSD. It also means that even though that person is unlikely to ask for help from you directly, that person still needs your help. You need to help this person understand their situation, which is likely to open up the person to the idea of getting help.

You need to approach this very carefully, slowly, and gently so that you do not offend or end up aggravating the person's pain and symptoms.

Let's talk about how you can go about this.

Chapter 11:
How to Help and Support Your Loved One Accept PTSD and Work towards Dealing with It

Helping someone struggling with PTSD come to terms with his/her problem and agree to get proper help is not easy. That said, it's something you need to instigate, and you can do that, provided you stay committed to the cause and take the following measures.

To help your loved one identify and accept PTSD, you can use the following measures to offer support as your loved one gradually works towards dealing with the root of the issue.

Establish Trust

If someone you are trying to help does not trust you, they will not believe you, even if you are telling the truth. You need to establish your loved ones' trust so that they accept what you say as the truth, and feel that they can place their faith in your love for them.

To establish trust, you need to spend as much time as you

can with your loved one, especially in moments where you feel that the person may need someone to listen to their feelings of pain.

You must also be truthful about whatever you discuss with the person, even if it is routine stuff. Never lie to your loved one so that they know you are honest and they believe you when you try to help them understand their PTSD signs.

Additionally, if and whenever your loved one shares their feelings about the pain and trauma they went through, or what they felt, do not share these stories with anybody else.

These are the person's confidential feelings and thoughts, and it is a huge deal for them to trust you with those sentiments. If you share what you know with others, you will break the person's trust long before it takes stable roots. Keep your promise of being a trustworthy friend/loved one, and they will always find you credible enough to accept your advice when you ask them to get help for their PTSD.

Moreover, once you build a relationship of trust with your loved one that is fighting the battle within, your loved one will likely want to keep you updated with the different symptoms they experience, allowing you to help them out.

Listen to Their Feelings

All of us have an innate need to feel validated and heard. Unfortunately, very few of us find that keen ear and a compassionate heart to pour out our sentiments to. When someone battles with PTSD, they often start to bottle up their feelings and thoughts. That's because the person often feels that nobody will understand them and because the person has no trusted confidant with whom to share these thoughts and feelings.

You can ask questions about why your loved one feels stuck in that episode, or how something made them feel, but pay attention to their facial expressions when you ask them any questions. In the case that they flinch or look upset or frown when you ask a question, change the course of the conversation. Apologize for hurting the person's sentiments and make it clear that should the person wish to end the conversation, you will understand. When you take this approach, it makes sure that your loved one feels comfortable instead of feeling pressured, which allows them to relax and open up to you in a calm pace that will prove to be beneficial.

When you become the confidant of the person you want to help, the person will start to accept your suggestions and opinions. This trust makes it possible to start helping that person slowly understand the symptoms of PTSD and the effects it has on their ability to live a good life.

At this point, you can suggest seeking professional help or following the different coping mechanisms discussed in this guide to manage their PTSD. Throughout this journey, be patient with the person you want to help so that he or she continues to share their thoughts with you, and you continue to offer direct guidance where doing so is necessary. Be their battle buddy.

Offer Reassurance

Reassurance is something all of us need when we go

through challenging times in our lives. Your friend who lost her partner who was shot while policing the streets, your elder brother who once served in the military, or your colleague who witnessed the death of his kids all want the same thing: reassurance!

If someone struggling with PTSD trusts you enough to open up to you about their feelings, offer reassurance. You don't need to paint overly positive and unrealistic pictures of why they should fight PTSD. Instead, give them realistic advice and simply help them understand how normal it is to feel this way and give them options on how to combat these issues.

Do not attempt to shun the person's feelings; simply tell them how it is natural to experience these thoughts. Talk about how mustering the courage to share their feelings with you is one of the bravest things you've ever seen. Make the person feel comfortable sharing with you.

Help the person understand that while it's normal and natural to feel this way, it is important to curb the matter because it interferes with routine life and functioning. Help the person go through the next section where I share the different effects of PTSD on one's body and mind so that they know how PTSD is slowly poisoning their wellbeing, sanity, and life.

Throughout this process, be gentle. Do not push your loved one to rush through the process, but especially avoid forcing your loved on to get therapy or try a remedy to curb PTSD.

If your friend talks to you about his feelings from days of service in the army, do not confront him about having PTSD or ask him to get help immediately. That is an irrational and hasty approach to helping your loved one, and can feel like coercion instead of help and support.

Once your loved one comes to terms with PTSD, keep talking to them about their feelings and just keep telling them how you value and respect their strength. After a few days of reassuring them, offer to accompany your loved one for a visit to someone who can help them with the matter. However, if your loved one dissents, do not bring up the topic again for a while.

Encourage Them to Seek Help Before it is Too Late

It is our responsibility as friends and family members to reach out if someone is in need or if someone is suffering and you can tell that they are suffering.

Don't let my story be your story:

I had a colleague who was suffering from it. Periodically, I would speak to him about everything that was going on and he confided in me and opened up about a lot of the stuff that was eating at him because I, too, had PTSD, and we both were prior military. We would talk about the VA and how we were getting treated and what medications we were taking, and all the details of our stories that made us the way we were.

Some sufferers want to self-medicate by drinking while others choose to abuse prescribed medication. When people self-medicate, often it is with alcohol and sometimes illicit drugs; in this case, my friend would drink himself to sleep. I would share with him my struggles with alcohol abuse the first few years I had PTSD before I even knew I had it. I would tell him stories about not being able to sleep and how nothing over-the-counter would help at all.

I would see him come in to work with sunglasses on at 6 a.m. when the sun was not even up, and I would ask him how late he stayed up the night before, and if he drank. His answer was always, "Come on man, you know what it is." Then he would lay back into his desk, and doze off. He was an awesome man who loved his family, his wife and his two baby girls. He was also very proud to have served his country honorably. My friend saw combat overseas and he saw some friends get their limbs blown up, he also saw some die.

An accumulation of all these things is not easy to let go; it is not easy to explain to somebody who has never been in such a position what and why something is bothering them the way it is, especially if you have no idea what that person went through and why they didn't want to speak to a counselor about it.

I had a few incidents in the military, and also as a policeman, where I saw people die and had a few friends die as well, so he knew that I understood what he was going through and that was mainly why we could open up to each other that way.

Somehow, I stopped drinking a lot just before I married my wife. I saw what the experience did to my previous fiancé and I did not want the same thing to happen with her. I knew when I drank it intensified my thoughts, and it also made me short-tempered, ready for an altercation at any time. When I stopped drinking, I no longer had to worry about what stupid stuff I did when I was drunk.

My friend was compelled by the police department to go back to patrol and leave our offices and the schedule that he had. When he left we would text for a few days and then the texting stopped. I didn't think anything of it, I honestly thought that he was just really busy with work and his family. I would shoot him a text here and there and I would receive very short responses.

To this day, I am ashamed of not being more proactive in reaching out to his wife or actually taking the time to call him and speak to him. One day I saw the news reporting an accident in which a car hit another car and killed the driver, and I remember saying to myself that the SUV on TV looked a lot like his car. I also realized that the accident was right next to where his house was so I immediately texted him to see if he was okay and I got no response. Then I heard the newscaster say that it involved a police officer who was under the influence of alcohol, and my heart dropped. I immediately knew it was him.

I called around to the other colleagues to ask if they knew the name of the officer; they did not know. Finally, they reported the name of the officer, and it was him. I didn't know the details of it, but I do know that he was intoxicated and that he was driving. He drifted onto an oncoming lane, and his vehicle collided with a car coming from the opposite direction, killing a man who was a single parent on his way to work. Fortunately, he did not die – but this new scar added to the ones that were already eating at him.

I knew that I had to speak to him, so I waited until he was bonded out. I called him and I could tell from his tone that he was not the same person. I tried to keep him in good spirits, but I knew with everything he was going through, including this latest incident, that it was a dangerous situation. After that initial conversation, I sent him text messages that he never responded to. I was waiting for the worst. After a while, I figured he was just going to wait it out, take his sentencing, and serve his time in jail.

One day before he was supposed to appear in court, his name came over the news again and this time, it was reported that he was found dead in his home, hanging by a rope.

As a grown man, there are times in your life when you ask yourself if you did everything possible to prevent an event from taking place. And at that moment, I felt like I didn't do enough. I cried because I knew I had the same feelings that he had. I have known the feeling of taking a life on more than one occasion, and it is an empty, helpless feeling - knowing you took out somebody's husband or father or friend or son.

Some people don't understand how it could get so bad that some will take their own life, but I can tell you firsthand it happens. And when it does, it is the lowest point of that person's life. I miss him like a brother and every time I think of him, I whisper how sorry I am that I didn't do more, into the air as if he is there listening.

Spot Red Flags

Depression is a brain illness that can be fatal if it goes without being treated for a long period of time. Sixteen million Americans are affected by depression every year. According to statistics, only 35.5% of people with depression seek help. Some are worried about the stigma and others are not thinking that it is a big deal; some even think it would be a sign of weakness to seek help. Depression is very hard to deal with alone. [Stats can be found at mhanational.org under depression.]

I think it is very important for family and friends to be able to spot out habits or signs of depression. This won't guarantee that the person will open up to you once you confront them about it, but it will show them that you are aware and concerned about them which will create an avenue for them to seek help when they're ready. Watch out for isolation. When I felt depressed, I would isolate myself from family and friends, ignoring calls from loved ones.

I didn't want anyone to see through me. I threw myself into working nonstop to keep my mind off of the trauma and when I got home, I would drink until I passed out. I became stressed out about why I was not able to get over the issues I had and it honestly made it worse for me. I would push people I loved away in anger for absolutely no reason.

Problems sleeping are a huge red flag as well. This affects physical and mental well-being. People suffering from this usually have negative thoughts running through their head constantly. When I dealt with this issue, I would literally get up and go to clubs because I couldn't sleep. This only led to me drinking more, making bad decisions, and then crashing at weird times of the day and sleeping through important meetings or appointments I needed to be at.

Some are the complete opposite and will stay in bed because their mental strength is weakened to the point where they have no energy at all. This will interfere in their daily routines and jobs as well.

Lack of energy is a huge factor. You will see them avoiding certain things they usually never avoid such as eating, showering and even socializing. Because of the lack of energy they will often not take care of their health and can end up gaining larger amounts of weight - this is what I went through. I just wanted to buy food on the way home and plop my fat ass in front of the television where I could forget everything in my life.

People suffering from depression often have distractions. These can be detrimental to your recovery.

Some distractions can help people focus on something more positive instead of dealing with the negative. For me, I had acquired bad distractions before I finally found the good ones. My bad distractions were drowning myself with alcohol in clubs and dating random women which brought on a whole other set of problems on its own. After dealing with the symptoms and going to multiple therapy sessions, I learned how to implement positive distractions in my life such as writing, reading, working out, listening to music, etc. These positive distractions can help keep the negative thoughts out of your head.

Depression is horrible and it tricks people into thinking that they're not loved, that life has no meaning, and that there's no reason to try. The hardest thing I did was try and cover it up- I always told everyone I was just tired and hoped they would brush it off after seeing that I worked a lot of hours. You should never be ashamed to reach out for help. Know that you are not alone and there are millions of people suffering from it as well.

With the right help, you can get your life back under control. I highly suggest the first stop should be your company's psychologist or spend your own money on an outside one and get a plan set up for you. If you are a veteran, please reach out to the VA and set up your appointments. It is worth it and your future self will thank you for it- trust me.

Remember that people's perception is their reality- it's up to us to show them how to improve their lives to be productive and happy again. When speaking to people who are depressed or suffering from these symptoms, it is important to remember that over 90% of communication is nonverbal, so be aware of your and their body language.

Supervisors and coworkers in all professions should reach out to people that are showing red flags. Dialogue with them to show that you care about what is going on and interested in helping them adjust to the changes they're experiencing.

When you speak to them, give them your full attention - leave your phone in your pocket and engage with the person making eye contact. When you speak to them, get them out of the work space, stay away from closed spaces or offices. Be aware of your body language and try not to seem closed off. Making this effort may open doors to create a more pleasant work environment and/or home life. People who are going through this will appreciate the concern and will also see that someone cares.

I would love to see more professions create a Peer Support system that is geared towards proactively reaching out to people who are struggling. This will identify people who need help and get them the help that's needed for them to get back on track to succeeding professionally and personally. By having a system that initiates this, it eliminates the pressure of them having to reach out and risk embarrassment or the perception of something being wrong with them by their peers.

During this process, there should not be any isolation

while they receive help that is needed. Since it is protocol in a lot of departments around the Nation for officers to be relieved of duty during any pending investigation, officers can naturally become separated from those that are used to leaning on for support. This can do more harm than good for some who suffer with PTSD if they are away from the comradery of their brothers and sisters in uniform, and in turn kept at home to be alone with their trauma. Keeping them engaged with the department and having them feel a sense of purpose will go a long way.

Remember, the goal is to get them healed and back doing what they do best: being productive and serving the citizens. We have to be there for each other and let them know that they are not alone. This will build a healthy workplace when they know the people they work for are there for them and their well-being.

> *"Telling the story was absolutely therapeutic for a long period of time. I didn't realize it, but one theory I have about why I think I don't suffer from most of the symptoms that would be associated with PTSD is that I have told this story."*
>
> ~Chief Warrant Officer Mike Durant (POW during Desert Storm)

Help the Person Understand the Effects of PTSD

You need to walk the person you are trying to help through the different implications and effects of PTSD on one's body, mind, and soul. This will ensure that the person fully comprehends how the condition is influencing them. Again, I will emphasize the importance of staying calm and gentle throughout the process.

Before going through the effects of PTSD, I would like to highlight the fact that since you will be working closely with someone going through PTSD, the experience is likely to be overwhelming for you as well. While you may not be struggling with PTSD, working, or even talking with someone suffering from the problem can make you feel as if you are going through the same condition too.

Also, at times, the person's symptoms may start rubbing off on you such that you find yourself losing your calm, becoming agitated, getting lost in thoughts, becoming edgy, etc. This realization can be quite overpowering for you, which is why you need to mitigate your stress daily.

It is crucial to find activities that bring you peace and integrate them into your daily routine. Even if it's just an hour it will help to relieve some stress and feel better.

Doing this helps keep your sanity in check so that you can stay calm and wear off your stress before it turns into something chronic. Additionally, when you are relaxed, you are more capable of helping your loved one battle PTSD. Remember to be consistent every day because little efforts yield compound results. Moreover, you will inspire your dear one to do the same, which will empower the person to deal with their PTSD.

Chapter 12:
Effects of PTSD on the Body and Mind

First, understand that PTSD symptoms start to develop due to a malfunctioning in the two main regions of your brain: the amygdala and prefrontal cortex (PFC). The amygdala is a tiny brain structure that looks like an almond. It rests deep in the center of the temporal lobe in the brain.

Its job is to detect different threats in your surrounding environment and set off the 'stress response' or the 'fight or flight' response in your body. It also activates the sympathetic nervous system that helps you manage threats and stores new memories pertinent to your emotions or threats.

The prefrontal cortex, on the other hand, is in the frontal lobe, right behind the forehead. Its role is to help you make decisions pertinent to a certain situation. It also helps regulate your awareness and attention, initiate voluntary behavior, determine the emotional importance and meaning of different events, correct or inhibit different dysfunctional reactions, and regulate your emotions.

When you encounter a threat, your brain detects it. Your amygdala then sets off an automatic 'fight or flight' response that involves the release of the hormones norepinephrine and adrenaline, along with glucose to energize your body and brain. If the threat continues, your amygdala communicates with the pituitary gland and hypothalamus (another region of the brain) to release cortisol in your body too. In the meantime, the medial portion of your prefrontal cortex assesses threats and calms down the 'stress response.'

Studies conducted on PTSD show that those struggling with the condition have a very hyperactive amygdala and a less activated medial PFC. that means if you or someone else is going through PTSD, they are likely to react intensely to a potential threat because of the overcharged amygdala.

Since PTSD impairs the functionality of the PFC system, the person will not be able to regulate their response to the threat. They are likely to continue experiencing the 'stress response' for a prolonged period. That is why a person may display symptoms of PTSD and continue to experience a state of fear and trauma for weeks or even months after the traumatic episode occurred.

Consequences of Different Brain Dysfunctions during PTSD

Let me now walk you through the different brain dysfunctions one can go through as they suffer from PTSD.

Hyper arousal

Because of the overcharged amygdala, more norepinephrine gets released into the bloodstream in response to a threatening situation. Since PFC cannot regulate the release of the hormone, it continues to circulate in the bloodstream for a long time. It then creates hyper-vigilance, hyper-arousal, and sleep disruptions, along with increased wakefulness.

Due to hyper-arousal, those going through PTSD become emotionally triggered by anything that tends to resemble their original trauma. For instance, if a survivor of a sexual assault is talking about their story, they may tense up upon someone touching them. The sight of a gun may emotionally trigger your best friend, who was once a police officer and nearly shot dead during a robbery he responded too.

Along with hyper-arousal, other things can make your loved one going through PTSD become on edge. Since the person has a high amount of norepinephrine in the body, it leads to wakeful nights in bed full of tossing and turning.

Tremors

Tremors stem from our triggers. According to Medicine. Net, a tremor is an involuntary, rhythmic muscle contraction leading to shaking movements in one or more parts of the body. Tremors are common in hands, arms, head, torso, and legs. They can occur sporadically on their own, or happen as a result of PTSD or another disorder like TBI (Traumatic Brain Injury), or stroke, alcohol abuse, and anxiety or panic attacks. All of these can be caused by PTSD. When pills don't work, a lot of us self-medicate and most turn to alcohol, while some turn to illegal drugs. I still suffer from tremors periodically in my eye lids, hands and legs. Many don't understand how they got to this point.

VA studies also assert that 76% of veterans experience

alcohol, drugs and mental health problems. Many are broken and feel like they have no hope, which is why they isolate themselves and want to be alone. This may give the perception to others that they are unapproachable.

Impulsivity and Reactive Anger

Since the amygdala is overly reactive, it keeps those battling PTSD on constant alert. They become hyper-alert and are always ready to take quick action the instant they sense something not right in the environment.

The orbital PFC is a region of the PFC that inhibits motor behavior, i.e., physical action when it is inappropriate. For instance, if your PFC is functioning properly, you are unlikely to jump with fear when you see a shadow, or you may not yell at your friend in the case that he forgets to call you on time as he promised. You know these are inappropriate behaviors, and your PFC helps you realize them and disengage from them.

However, in someone going through PTSD, their orbital PFC has very low volumes and is under-active. That means that those going through PTSD have very little control over their impulsive behaviors; they often react with anger or fear every time they feel emotionally triggered. Both of these behaviors tend to interfere with one's routine functioning, performance, and relationships.

Decreased Positive Emotionality and Increased Fear

Individuals battling PTSD tend to experience an excess

amount of negative emotions. They find it difficult to enjoy their daily activities and social interactions. Perhaps your loved one struggling with PTSD has lost interest in activities that they once enjoyed doing. It could be because of the hyperactive amygdala that influences their medial PFC that is making it difficult for them to regulate emotions.

Help your loved one understand that all these effects heavily influence their daily life can have the following implications:

- They are likely to lose their calm around loved ones, venting out their frustrations on others.
- Their relationships start to become strained as PTSD takes a toll on them.
- Their work performance lowers as their focus and productivity continues to drop to exceedingly low levels.
- They lose interest in life.
- They become lethargic and are likely to feel exhausted all the time.
- They start to isolate themselves from people and may sink into depression and anxiety.
- They become very suspicious of people and find it hard to trust others, which keeps them from forming new, healthy relationships and strengthening the existing ones.
- They hardly sleep well, which takes a toll on their mental and physical health.
- They are unable to connect to their spiritual side and find out what their life purpose is.
- They feel restless all the time.

These problems won't let your loved one live peacefully, which is why you ought to encourage your loved one to seek treatment for PTSD. [marylandrecovery.com] [brightquest.com] [healthyplace.com]

Chapter 13:
Seeking Support for PTSD and Controlling Symptoms

We have different associations and forums that you or your loved one that is battling PTSD can use to seek help and support. The American Psychiatric Association is a certified association that provides different programs that offer relief from PTSD. Additionally, you can conduct a quick search on various PTSD support programs online and find a suitable one for yourself or your loved one.

Most of these programs consist of medication and mindfulness-based techniques. These two approaches decrease the volume of the amygdala and improve the connectivity between the PFC and the amygdala. This enhanced connectivity calms the amygdala and enables the PFC to respond better to a threatening situation.

You or your loved one can try any of the following strategies:

Deep Breathing

You need to learn how to start breathing deeply by

inhaling from your nose and exhaling through the mouth to a count of 5 every time you feel scared or triggered. Practicing deep breathing for a mere 5 minutes can help you calm down enough to be able to take charge of your irrational thoughts.

Stay focused and be calm and collected during stressful situations. Practice speaking in a calm tone whether on the radio to relay information or to yourself under your breath.

By doing this, you will notice your focus will be directed towards what needs to be said rather than the actual trauma you are witnessing. This will lessen issues that may harm you or others such as getting too excited, not being able to control your breathing, getting angry, or making the wrong decisions. Controlling your tone and what you say will make you hold all that in and get everything under control.

This will have you focusing on what needs to be said or done. The mental strength it takes from doing this will help you control your pulse, breathing, and emotions. This will help you assess the situation and allow you to assist in rescuing others and be an asset rather than someone who may be a hindrance to the situation. This also helps when you are going through episodes after the incident as well.

I can remember when I would wake up screaming after a vivid dream drenched with sweat and my heart pounding in my chest while I tried to catch my breath. I would repeat three things I am grateful for over and over again out loud - each time I would make a conscious effort to control my tone and my breathing. Usually, after a few minutes of this, I was calm and my shaking or other side effects would go away as well.

This would also work when I would get set off by a

trigger- in my case seeing large knives kicked my body and mind into panic mode and I would start to literally lose my breath and sweat uncontrollably while my heart would try to jump out of my chest. During these times, I learned to focus my attention on those three things I was most grateful for at the time and I would repeat these things while I focused on my breathing until I calmed down. I would also sometimes count out loud to ten with a deep breath for every number that was said, while holding my hands behind my head to straighten out my airway. Before I started doing these coping techniques, an incident like this would screw up my entire day and also make me irritable and not pleasant to be around. This allowed me to move on with my day with a positive feeling knowing that I have things to live for.

Mindfulness

Learn the art of living mindfully by consciously focusing on the task at hand. For example, if reading a book, ensure the focus is on the words so that you are mindfully bringing all awareness to the content of the book. Cultivating mindfulness takes time and dedication. A great way to adopt this ability is to commit to reminding yourself to stay mindful of each moment.

Gratitude

As you do this, make sure to consciously count and acknowledge all the blessings in your life. It could be loving friends, shelter, clothes to wear, etc. The more you focus on them, the easier it becomes for you to start seeing the proverbial light at the end of the tunnel even when you experience PTSD symptoms.

Faith & Family

While I personally am still on my own journey of discovering what my faith looks like, I have seen a number of religious organizations provide support for those suffering from PTSD. Whether it is through hosting AA meetings, or just providing people with a sense of community, being connected with a church can help those who struggle with PTSD to have hope even when they feel hopeless. Additionally, I cannot stress enough the importance of family. I am fortunate to have a strong family support system, but I have to be the one that chooses to not isolate myself and believe that they love me or want the best for me. If you do not have a good relationship with your biological family, I encourage you to take the time to consider who could be your family in this season- people you can open up to and lean on as you journey toward recovery.

Acceptance

Moreover, understand that what happened in the past happened, and since no one can go back in time, getting worked up over it is in no way beneficial to anyone. Create a mental image of that episode and then burst that bubble while taking deep breaths. This exercise helps you to calm down and make peace with the episode.

Self-Care

Taking care of yourself physically and emotionally is imperative to a healthy recovery. When you experience trauma, your mind is not in the right state to be able to operate and function effectively. In my experience, either your home life or your work life will take the hit-in my case it was both.

Your mind is a muscle that needs to be hardened - trauma can do this to you in instances that are actually good for you in terms of survival and how your mind will react to the next incident that may happen. However, a lot of people deal with depression, anger, hopelessness, and other symptoms from PTSD.

What helped me slowly form a shield from these symptoms was self-development. I know what you're thinking-oh Lord, another motivational guy. That's not what I am or what I want to be. Listening and reading about how others got through their troubles equips you with an arsenal of weapons to combat PTSD symptoms and helps you live your life better for you, your loved ones.

I wake up at least an hour before I need to start getting ready for my day and usually put on my headphones and listen to an audio book or YouTube video of a topic that I'm dealing with at the time. If there is not a specific topic that I am struggling with that day, I will use that time to listen to a video or audiobook on a skill or a topic I would like to learn more about. Doing this sets my mind to a learning mode and focuses my attention on whatever I am learning about and leaves no room for my mind to drift back to my dark places and it starts my day in a positive light. Listening to these videos or audiobooks will also help you want to change for the better and give you a sense of purpose, which we all need.

Taking cold showers brings in way more benefits and results than you would think. Taking cold showers speeds up your metabolism and wakes you up a lot faster. It lowers your body's temperature which allows you to burn off more calories, boosts your heart rate, and improves your blood circulation. This can help ease stress on a physical and an emotional level. For men, it will boost their testosterone which is great in fending off anxiety and depression.

One small thing I did was change my picture on my phone every week with something that I need to live for. One week would be a picture of my fiancé who is now my wife, the next would be my mother, and I would keep changing them as the weeks went by. Every now and then, if I ran across a saying that caught my attention, I would use that as my screensaver as well, so I could have something that changed my thought process when I felt stressed.

Little changes like this in your everyday life will help you stay out of a depressed state. Some people even write inspirational quotes on paper and tape it to their mirrors in their homes so they see it right when they wake up and every time they look at themselves. One of my particular favorites is "Exhaust yourself physically to recover emotionally"- George S. Everly PhD.

Find ways to work the stress off. This could be anything outdoors or anything that you have to push yourself through.

Sweat it out! During this time, I went to the gym and let out all my anger on the weights and I would also do cardio to wear myself out. I also used to disappear to Galveston, because I found that the water and the wind that came off the beach soothed me and relaxed my mind. Sometimes I would even run on the beach and get a work out there while taking in the scenery and the sounds of the beach. Afterwards, I would sit there for hours by myself staring out into the water thinking about ways to get myself back on track. I found this to be very helpful in my recovery.

Find an outlet and use it continuously in your everyday life. This could be fishing, sports, and the gym, visiting the beach, or running. Not only will finding a hobby take your mind off of the negative thoughts, it will also exhaust you to where you can hopefully sleep a little better at night.

Journaling

Accountability is key to recovery - be truthful to yourself. I learned in therapy that keeping a journal was the best thing I could ever do. Every morning when I woke up, I would write out what I needed to do for the day along with short term goals. Throughout the day or at the end of it, I would cross out the things I accomplished on the list. During the day, I would use it as a marker to show me what needed to be done so I didn't have down time where my mind would drift.

I would also use this journal to leave detailed notes on what I experienced throughout the day and night and I would time stamp them as well. While you list these details, don't leave out your feelings that you are dealing with during these episodes. This is important to track because if the level of anxiety or depression you're experiencing is gradually getting better, then you know you are on the right path, and if they're not, then you know you may have to change a few things around or seek more professional help to address this. Doing this helps you keep track of what is going on with you and you can also see if you are getting better or worse over time.

Keeping a detailed journal will also help your therapist get a better picture of what's going on with you. This will allow them to know your stressors and how to form their therapy to fit your needs. Doing this will save a lot of money on therapy sessions because they will spend less time digging stuff out of you and more time focusing on how to deal with your problems.

Know that everything you do when you are suffering from PTSD (Post Traumatic Stress Disorders) matters. Every little victory you have in your life matters and it will have a huge impact in your recovery. Every time you cross something off your list in your journal that is considered a win that will push you to the next goal on your list. When you start conquering more things on a daily basis, it will simultaneously boost your morale and sense of self-worth. Improving your self-esteem will make you more open to other recovery techniques. Stick to your plan and execute it; this is the only way to see drastic changes.

If you or your loved one implements these approaches, soon enough, you will have control over the PTSD symptoms. Besides these strategies, you also need to understand that learning from and leaning on others is one of the best ways to overcome challenges. From my own personal experience and the victories I have had, I created a Battle Buddy podcast so that those dealing with PTSD can share their stories, what works for them, and ultimately let others know that they are not alone.

BATTLE BUD

P O D C A S T

A Conversation with a combat veteran

Charles

Charles and I went through elementary, junior high, and high school together. We also played football together. Charles and I also left for the service around the same time, so to say that Charles and I have a lot in common would be an understatement.

Unfortunately, after coming back from the service, we lost touch for a while. Fortunately, we later reconnected, and I'm so glad that happened. Charles is doing some very interesting things to help veterans and cops manage and overcome PTSD: he's training dogs, called K-9 battle buddies, for veterans. Here is an overview of our interview:

"Why do veterans and those recovering from PTSD need dogs?"

165

Various studies have shown that people who experience symptoms of Post-Traumatic Stress Disorder and anxiety can benefit from having a companion in the form of a dog.

For instance, a 2015-2016 research study funded by Bayer Animal Health and the Human-Animal Bond Research Institute (HABRI) concluded that, overall, veterans and cops who had a service dog experienced lower PTSD symptoms. In this specific study, out of a pool of 141 participants, all of whom were veterans, the 76 that had service dogs showed an enhanced ability to cope with the symptoms of PTSD.

Besides that, Dogs are natural PTSD healers because they are companionable; they make great battle buddies. Additionally, they have a keen ability to sense the build-up of anxiety or anger in their owners —or whoever has the dog at that particular time.

The service dogs used as PTSD companions go through training that helps them know how to react in a manner that ensures their owner starts calming down, and gets back to a normal state of mind.

Charles works for an organization called TADSAW: Train a Dog, Save a Warrior, an organization that's training dogs to save veterans struggling with PTSD.

https://tadsaw.org/

During our conversation, Charles noted that the number of veterans that kill themselves a day had jumped from 22 to 26. He also stated that TADSAW aims to facilitate veterans acquiring well-trained service dogs that can help them handle and overcome symptoms of PTSD when they need it the most. He noted:

"For veterans that don't have a dog that's ready for an evaluation or special training, we can then go to a shelter and find a battle buddy. I always say that "dog" spelled backward reads "God," which makes a lot of sense to me because a dog will always be there for you."

When Charles mentioned the word Battle Buddy, since that's the title of my podcast, I got extremely curious. I wanted to learn how he —as a veteran— and TADSAW as an organization, define the term, especially to someone who lacks military experience, which is where the use of the phrase is most common.

Battle Bud: What It Means

This is part of the reason why I choose the phrase as the name of my podcast. A battle bud, which is short for a battle buddy, is someone who is always there for you. It's someone who's always ready to go to battle by your side, and who sticks by you no matter how tough the going gets.

Charles has a similar understanding of the phrase. When I asked him to explain the phrase to any non-military listeners on my podcast, he had this to say:

"Okay. Let's see. A battle buddy to me is someone who would keep me out of trouble and vice versa during my time in service. Whether we went out to a bar, in public, field exercises, or paratrooper missions, a battle buddy was somebody to watch your back when you jumped from the aircraft...."

"Your battle buddy is somebody who has your back and is always going to have your back. When I was married, my wife

was my battle buddy. That's what having a battle buddy means: having someone looking out for you, making sure you're good, making sure they call you...."

"When dealing with PTSD and traumatic brain injuries, having a battle buddy, someone who calls to make sure you're okay, is critical. For example, I'm a battle bud to all the brothers I served with. Because of that, I often call them to make sure they're fine. During the call, we often do a sit-rep, which is a situation report just to see how we're doing. A battle bud is somebody who has and will always have your back no matter what."

As someone who's worked through PTSD —and is still on the life-long path to managing it— I know how important it is to have support from someone who's always ready to help you through the toughest of battles. And yes, PTSD is one of the hardest battles most veterans will have to fight.

Dogs as Battle Buds

The idea of having a battle bud, more so in the form of a dog, intrigued me. I asked Charles about how he got started as a K-9 dog trainer for veterans, as well as whether he had a K-9 battle buddy. To that, he stated:

"Yeah, I do. I have a service animal. His name is Dozer, like a bulldozer.

"...Back in 2013, I was trying to go to PTSD rehabilitation in Waco, Texas, but because I didn't have a battle buddy, someone looking out for me, and my now-ex-wife and I were having problems and issues, the prospect was very challenging. I

would often go to the rehab center, leave, then come back a few more times, before leaving again."

"{Out of the realization that I needed help, and out of a desire to get better,} I started looking into and researching service animals, which is how I learned about TADSAW, a San Antonio-based organization that was training dogs to save a warrior. "I reached out and filled out all the necessary paperwork."

I've had dogs all my life. I've also trained many dogs, but before contacting and later joining TADSAW, I did not know that service dogs could become PTSD companions. Before I started attending therapy sessions, which I did because I wanted to figure out what was going on with me and determine whether the pain and anguish I was feeling would ever go away, I didn't think PTSD was a real thing."

After filling out my paperwork with TADSAW, my dog and I went into training, which normally takes six months; that's how long it takes to train a service dog. The training provided by TADSAW taught my dog how to be a service animal and me how to be a trained service dog handler.

Although the training was not easy, and I had to do all the work, I'm glad I did because now I'm the trainer for the Texas branch of Veterans of Foreign Wars (VFW). Because I'm now a trainer, I'm at a point where I can willingly look for and help veterans who are serious about seeking help and going through the training that allows them to have a K-9 battle bud.

Besides training dogs and equipping them with the skills they need to become service animals, I also work with veterans and teach them how to get back to the state of mind they used *to have before joining the service.*

[Most people] don't realize this, but before going into service, veterans had normal, rich lives; they were outgoing. They also don't realize that when you get into service, life becomes about having a battle buddy and being a battle buddy to all the other brothers and sisters in service with you.

{They} also don't realize that when people come out the other end of military service, they lose something important: the camaraderie that everybody lives for and the sense of purpose they had with their battle buddies in service. To veterans, being in service often feels like traveling at 300 miles per hour, which is okay because while in service, you have a battle bud, someone who has your back, but when we get out of service, we often feel stuck. At {TADSAW} we use dogs to help veterans find a purpose and a healthy outlet for their PTSD symptoms."

On a personal level, I know the importance of having a healthy outlet for PTSD symptoms. From personal experience, I know that without an outlet, we're likely to give into the temptation to use self-medication as an outlet. This type of coping mechanism can potentially lead to behavioral problems, issues with the law, or even other worst-case scenarios.

I also know the importance of having a purpose, especially to someone going through PTSD. I know that if you don't have a purpose in life, especially coming out of the military where every day we had a purpose, dealing with the disorder can be incredibly challenging.

While in the force, the purpose is to keep each other and the country safe. Life outside the force is incredibly different. Without the sense of purpose that comes from being in the force, nor the camaraderie of having fellow brothers and sisters in uniform, dealing with PTSD and its symptoms can be immensely challenging.

Having a sense of purpose is an especially effective way to manage and overcome PTSD. That's because having a sense of purpose gives you a mission, a goal, or something to work towards.

On Joining the Military & Stories from the Service

As Charles and I talked more on the podcast, we eventually got to talking about joining the force and sharing our stories.

As it turned out, Charles got into military service in 2002 at the age of 22, and got out in 2010 at the age of 30, which is also when I got in and out too.

"... I got into some trouble after high school, not legal stuff or anything. But, I found myself going out partying and doing unhealthy things. At that point, even though I was barely out of high school, I knew a life of drinking wasn't it for me. I went into service in July of 2002. I consider that hands-down the best decision I have ever made."

During our conversation, I asked Charles to describe to my non-military listeners what it was like to go into the military, and the mindset he was operating from as he made the decision to enroll. I also asked him to share what life was like in and after the military.

To that, he replied:

"...One thing I'm going to say is that the decision to join

was the easiest one I've ever made because everybody else was either going in the military, jail, or to college. I wanted to join to do something and also to check out what it was like to travel and see things out of the ordinary. Joining sounded amazing, so I did."

"...I joined up, not knowing I would go to war. I didn't even think twice about it. A lot of people say, 'thank you for your service, but you made that choice to do it yourself.' They are 100 percent accurate; we decided to join, but when you are in combat, it changes you no matter what friends you have in the military."

Something most people don't realize is 22 is a very young age for someone to jump into a situation where they have to see combat and life and death situations almost daily. Those kinds of experiences can leave a lasting effect on one's psyche.

To veterans, the decision to enroll is life-changing. Charles agreed with me on that by noting:

"Yeah, definitely. It's life-changing, more so when you enroll and learn about the battle buddy system. The battle buddy system proves really effective whenever you're in a country where all you have are your brothers and sisters in uniform."

"{in such situations}, it's easy to feel stuck, more so when you're doing the same thing 24 hours a day, seven days a week for however long you're stationed. Initially, they told us it was going to be for 30 days; then, the 30 days become another 30, and then another, and before we knew it, we'd been deployed for 50 months in the desert."

"...During enrollment, we traveled through many dangerous routes and back highways. I especially remember

Highway 8, now called the All American Highway, because it was one of the deadliest highways in Iraq. Being part of that 2003 mission that became a Time Magazine Feature felt good. However, being in an atmosphere where the only way to survive was to do what you needed to do was not easy. It definitely created something."

"...I'll say this, when I came back from that mission and deployment, I thought I was untouchable. I had a sense of entitlement, a feeling that because I'm a combat veteran, people owed me something. I held on to that notion for a really long time, and it ended up creating a gap between my family and my friends.

"... At times like those, you definitely know who's loyal to you and who you are loyal to. When we come back, most people look at us like we're crazy. In reality, when you do whatever you can to survive when you're in a war, you have to bring that back, and you have to find a way to let that go. It's very hard to do, and as I'd said earlier, it's either in jail, college, or in the military. Once you come back, you're never going to be the same as the person you were before you left.

Hearing this caused me to think about how life in the military changed me; it also inspired me to ask Charles to narrate to my audience how being in service changed him. To that, he noted:

"... I was never a drinker when I went in. I learned how to drink and how to party while I was in the military. When I got out of the military, I didn't know what PTSD was. They had an acronym for it, Post Traumatic Stress Disorder. I didn't realize that it's a traumatic brain injury. We got into some stuff over *there that was pretty traumatic and unforgettable."*

Because I've had my fair share of trauma, and because the Battle Bud Podcast is about sharing trauma stories as a way to bring about PTSD awareness, I asked Charles to elaborate and give my listeners an idea of the kind of traumatic events he experienced, to which he replied:

"We saw a lot of IED and RPG around that time. I remember running over an IED while in a fast-moving vehicle, an ammo support tank. The RPG blew us from probably about, I'm going to say, six inches off the ground. You have an MCO, you have a driver, and then you have two guys. The gunner on top falls down. That was the E6. We had over probably 5,000 rounds. It all burnt off and popped off inside of it. That's one instance."

"...Everybody lived that day, which was good, but the traumatic part comes from the explosion. I don't know if you've ever been confronted with an EID, but the first thing you see is a white line followed by a big explosion, and you hope and pray to God that you're alive after that. That is an extremely scary experience. It's something that nobody wants to talk about." My grandfather, he died in 2015, may he rest in peace. He was the only one I could speak to about certain situations.

Veterans now have different outlets, such as the VFW, which is for veterans of foreign war, that they can use to seek help. To join, you have to be a combat veteran and a member of that cause.

My personal experience, however, was that they were doing the same thing: all they talked about was overcoming drugs. For me, being in that environment made the drinking *worse and worse.*

I remember waking up one morning and realizing that I had a bottle of liquor in the freezer and beer in the refrigerator, but no food. That was probably 2010. In 2011, I went to college."

Therapy Helps

"...I started college at Texas University. That's when I started finding out what my symptoms were. I was super hyper-vigilant. I was isolated. I was depressed. I didn't understand what these feelings and impulses were because I hadn't felt them before. I started going to therapy. Many people often talk about how you're less of a man because you go to therapy. Well, I beg to differ because therapy really helps; therapy and certain classes that they should take. They coincide with each other, and those things make you find out who you really are. And if anyone says that therapy is for a weaker person, you have to consider the source who said that.

You can't be afraid of what somebody else thinks. You know that you have to find what is making your heart and your mind be paranoid and hyper-vigilant in shutting down and not wanting to **** and not going in to prowl in certain situations."

Identify Triggers

From personal experience, I know that the best way to manage PTSD is to understand yourself well enough to be able to identify your triggers.

The only way to overcome PTSD symptoms is to educate

yourself on what exactly you have, and that's what I try to tell my listeners too. A lot of people haven't been through trauma, or they have no sense of direction for how to understand what they have.

That's why I've made it my mission in life to reach out to trauma victims that are open to sharing their story and experiences because we must help each other out like battle buddies to our listeners that haven't been through this stuff or that are going through it right now.

The ultimate goal is that they understand that they're not alone in this. Other people have done it, and other people are thriving now after the fact. You are going to have to deal with PTSD for the rest of your life, but you can learn to manage it. We can learn about what we have, and learn to know ourselves better. When we do this, we can stay away from the triggers and be more aware of coping skills we can utilize in those moments. On the importance of identifying triggers, Charles agreed with me and noted:

"Absolutely. You have to be mindful of those triggers that you were talking about. You have to be able to control what some people can't control and eventually get to the bottom of it, okay. It's really hard for a man or woman to find out who they really are. It's hard when you lay in bed at night time, and you close your eyes, and you're afraid to be in the room. You know what I'm saying? I've had six brothers and three died over there, and three committed suicide when they came back."

The reason why I wrote the book in the first place is that a friend I was really close to and I had worked with daily committed suicide. I knew he was going through stuff, and he knew I was too. We were taking the same kind of meds. We always spoke about how we were feeling. We were really each other's battle buddy.

We had just gotten a new chief. The new chief pulled him and put him back on the street because we were low on officers on the street. He was the lowest man on the totem pole type thing seniority wise, and that change happened within three days.

He was mainly going on day shift, weekends off, and being able to spend all of his time with his family, then he went into a totally different setting, with changed hours and his days off. Now, he was only able to see his family at certain times of the day, and even then, they were tired and ready to go to sleep. He didn't see a way out of it, so he started drinking again. I kind of lost touch with him because I didn't see him every day. Whenever I would text him or call him, he always gave really short responses. I sensed that something was wrong whenever that started happening. I felt that I needed to start calling him more often, but before I could, I saw in the news that he'd gotten in an accident and killed somebody.

For those of you who don't know what complex PTSD is, it is when a bunch of traumatic events occurs, and that creates multiple PTSD symptoms instead of just one traumatic event. He had multiple. He was in the Army. He went to war, and he got blown up too. He was under attack at night on his base. He had multiple traumas that were piling up, and then with this on top of it, it was just out of control. It was hard for me to reach out to him because I didn't want to overstep my boundaries. He's a grown man, so I didn't want to push myself onto him, which, now looking back, I should have. I should have gone over there, and I should have sat down with him and talked to him at his house.

Learn To Let Go of Things

After hearing my story, Charles gave me another important secret to overcoming PTSD: learning to let go of things, which is foundationally important. He noted:

"... you cannot hold onto that {pain.} One thing I've learned with my experiences is you have to learn to let go of things. Doing that is not easy, especially when the person you want to help does not seem to want help, but learning to let go is something we all need to learn."

"... As a battle buddy, you want to make sure you've tried everything: phone call, going over there, trying everything in your power to do that, and now you have to live with that guilt, and that's not fair. It's not fair."

I've learned to come to terms with my trauma. The way I'm dealing with it is through podcasting and writing books that help spread PTSD awareness. That way, the family members of people that are going through symptoms like that can see those red flags and get them the help they need before it's too late. Even if it helps to save just one life, I have done my job.

Create awareness

I wrote this book and started the Battle Bud podcast to create awareness because creating awareness is the first step to overcoming PTSD.

Charles agreed with me on the importance of awareness and is spreading it in his unique way. When I asked him where he's based now and what he's been doing, he noted:

"...I'm in Fort Worth. I sold my motorcycle, and then I bought an RV. I travel around now, and I spread awareness when I can, which is pretty much every day because I do my training every day. As I said, I like people to be aware of PTSD.

There are things that I can say to another veteran. We can talk to each other without offending each other. That is holding someone accountable for their actions. You have to be vulnerable for one to find these things out, and then you have to set boundaries on certain aspects of life. When you do that, the world is yours. It's yours."

Self-Education and Therapy

As Charles and I continued to talk, I eventually asked him if there was something specific, perhaps a certain book, a person, or a group that helped him overcome trauma, and that he could recommend to my listeners who were interested in self-education.

To that, he noted:

"Last year, or it was probably a year and a half ago, I heard of this guy called Nicholas Koumalatsos. They used to call him Marine Red Raider. He wrote a book called Excommunicated Warrior. The book is 190 pages long.

This is the best book I have ever read in years. The

book mainly talks about the seven transitions of life, the role of emotions, things like that. That book saved my life.

The book has been so impactful in my life that I even went on Facebook Messenger and messaged Nicholas Koumalatsos. Surprisingly, he messaged me back, which was great because it wasn't some super rock star that lacked credibility; he was just trying to get his name out there. After messaging back and forth, Nicholas even took the time to help me set goals and plans. In the book, Nicholas talks about climbing your mountain and how you have to make sure you get to the top.

I've been in therapy since 2009. That is something I absolutely believe in because the right therapist can hold you accountable. He or she can become your accountability partner and help you get to the root of the problem.

Let me use an analogy to help you understand. PTSD is a lot like an Iceberg. If you look at an iceberg, it appears to be melting away at the top. Underneath that iceberg, however, and underneath the water is another strong iceberg.

Most veterans, especially combat veterans, often feel like they've been through the wringer; they often feel like ducks on a pond. Everything looks cool and calm on top, but underneath, those feet are just kicking away 90 miles an hour. It's important to make sure you hold yourself to a level. To stay out of the bars and to avoid drugs, you have to be willing to step out of your comfort zone and find out who you are."

On a personal level, I know the importance of therapy. It definitely helped me out, but for years, I didn't find the right therapist. Eventually, I discovered a Post Critical Incident Seminar through LEMIT (Law Enforcement Management

Institute of Texas), and it changed my life. It was a turning point in recovery because it taught me how to separate myself from the incident and allows you to see why you're feeling everything you're feeling and why you're thinking a certain way. It gives you options. It often feels like someone has just lifted a bag of bricks off your shoulders. You learn how to look at an incident from an outside perspective, at the time I can remember thinking that this was total BS but shit, it worked. It works.

I was fortunate that my department paid for me to go to a session at Sam Houston State University; the seminar was four days, and we stayed at the school hotel overnight. There were 12 officers from all around Texas. We were in a circle telling our stories and then one by one over the course of four days, the instructor would take us into another room, and it would be a one on one session. This was four days of it. It worked wonders. I'm telling you, it was crazy.

Before the class, I would wake up swinging, get out of bed, and walk around the house multiple times a week. After the class, it dialed down a lot. Although I still have dreams and nightmares, they're not as intense. With EMDR (Eye Movement Desensitization and Reprocessing) and regular therapy professional and personal, I'm able to manage PTSD.

Support Is Key

My wife (who was then my girlfriend) went with me to the seminar held at Sam Houston. I'm definitely blessed to have her because she brought calmness to my world. I can never fully repay her for that. She has had a lot of patience and understanding for the toll that my kind of work has had on my mental health. But on my own, even before I eventually got into therapy, I had begun some effort to be more present with my loved ones too. Spending a larger portion of my free time with them was in itself therapeutic.

When I first joined the police department, I was engaged, and she was a great woman, but I totally screwed that up because I didn't understand how to control myself, my symptoms, or any of it. I didn't even know I had PTSD. I didn't know what PTSD was at all, and it wasn't until later that I did, but by then, the damage was already done.

As our conversation neared its end, I asked Charles to share something with the listeners, a piece of advice that he knew would help someone going through PTSD and feeling lost-here is what he had to say:

Be Bold

"I'm going to say don't be afraid to take that step. Don't be afraid to reach out. You have to make sure that if you notice something is wrong with you, or if you have an inclination that something's wrong or off with a family member or friend, don't be afraid to take that next step in asking for help. Asking for help is one of the most vulnerable and dangerous things any of us can do. It's dangerous because people are afraid to ask for help because they don't want to look weak. They don't want to look scared or anything like that. So, be strong." Asking for help is the most courageous thing someone can do. It's one of the most courageous things because vulnerability is a hard thing. Being

vulnerable is an extremely hard thing."

You can get a hold of me for service dog training. We will come out to you. We will find trainers in the area that will come and evaluate your dog. If you don't have a dog, we'll make sure that you are taken care of. We'll go to the local shelter, and 99 percent of the time, the dog finds you."

As I'd mentioned earlier, Charles and I grew up together. During the podcast, I discovered things I didn't know about PTSD. I realized that combat veterans experience the worst of the worst: they deserve all the respect we can give them!

If you would like to get in touch with Charles and get connected to his organization and K-9 training, you can email him at goosby52@gmail.com

Conclusion

The fact that military personnel and police officers do not know when to talk about their problems is very concerning. According to VA studies, we lose around 22 veterans a day to suicide, which comes to 7400 veterans every year committing suicide. Seventy percent of those veterans had no record of ever receiving any prior help.

Me with my family

According to Bluehelp.org there were 142 officers who committed suicide in 2016, 169 in 2017 and 169 in 2018. This year through October 2019 there are already 169 officers who have taken their own life and the year is not even finished yet. Some of the other lethal stressors are relationship issues, financial problems and legal problems such as being under investigation at the job and forced to wait at home for the verdict. We are not good at asking for help because military personnel and police officers are seen as strong and unapproachable by the public and our brothers and sisters in uniform. This holds us back from reaching out. This way of thinking has become part of the culture, and it must change in order to save the lives of our heroes who save the lives of others in our communities on a daily basis.

There are things that both the military and police departments take away from you and never put back. The first thing is empathy, which is the ability to care about what someone else is feeling. While this is effective in combat or dealing with hardened criminals, it is not effective in your marriage or dealing with your family and friends. This can make you want to isolate yourself from others in order to protect them from what you are saying, or if you are doing something that may offend them.

It is true that neither military nor police fear death but allowing needless deaths due to despair is not ideal for the society at large. Many of us have felt or encountered near-death experiences through the casualties we see on a regular basis. To now add the mental toll of dealing with the after-effects of our encounters is debilitating. The results leave some with having difficulty in finding a reason to live. What makes it worse is when these officers mention that they have issues they are grappling with, they often experience negative reactions from others in our profession.

A lot of us work on ourselves to build an emotional numbness in order to deal with the killings and casualties that we often witness. It also takes away the comfort in being able to ask for help; consequences are real in our fields of work. For example, both military and police departments could declare you medically unfit for duty. Both can have your guns taken away from you and both could have you taken away from your unit or take you off the streets where you patrol. To have your work and life taken away would be devastating. You could also be assigned a desk job, which is one of the most undesirable assignments on the force for officers that are accustomed to patrol or a specialized division.

As a community, we need to help our brothers suffering from the symptoms of PTSD see and recognize the reasons for living. Our loved ones say we look the same, but if they could see what's inside of us, it would scare the shit out of them. While they cheered for us when we came home from war or when we received awards as police officers, all I could do was just stare into a darkness of death and questions of why I was getting recognized for what I've done. For the longest time, I dealt with feelings of confusion and self-conflict. Although I sought help and it benefited me greatly, there are thousands of other brothers and sisters who were taught how to put their uniform on, but never taught how to take it off. They are here, still fighting to stay alive. I can still hear the screams of dying men and I can still smell very distinct smells of my gun going off. These memories have conflicts so deeply within them that many feel they will never win. Most are eaten up with sadness, never letting anybody in. And in doing so, it makes it hard for loved ones to recognize the person they knew before.

We try to live a normal life, but sometimes these triggers get the best of us until we seek the help that's needed. Triggers are anything that reminds you and puts you back into the moment you fear the most from your past experiences. For me, I have recognized my triggers. The sound of gunshots, large knives, large bodies of water, men screaming, large amounts of blood, wood breaking, and the anniversaries of those traumatic incidents are all triggers for me. Once we identify our triggers, we can learn to heal ourselves and each other.

It is up to us, the veterans, active military, and active and retired police officers, to educate the public on what their colleagues, loved ones, and neighbors who are going through trauma so we can assist in the recovery of our heroes who risk their lives for us overseas and within our communities. We have to let our trauma heal others that are going through hard times. You can't help others until you help yourself.

My wife and I

Finally, I want to thank my family for sticking by me through the hard times, and my wife who made a huge impact on my recovery by making a home for me and bringing a calmness to my world.

It is my hope that these short stories open your eyes and your heart to giving first responders all the backing and support they can get. I hope that by starting a conversation about PTSD awareness, we can remove the stigma it carries in the public and in the workplace. I believe peer support, whether it is in a working environment or within the family, will help those suffering get through their dark days and may prevent bad choices that could lead to imprisonment, ruining relationships and suicides.

This book was written in remembrance of my fallen brothers and sisters in and out of uniform, who fell victim to the battle within.

Resources

https://www.mayoclinic.org/diseases-conditions/post-traumatic-stress-disorder/symptoms-causes/syc-20355967
https://www.nimh.nih.gov/health/topics/post-traumatic-stress-disorder-ptsd/index.shtml
https://adaa.org/understanding-anxiety/posttraumatic-stress-disorder-ptsd/symptoms
https://www.webmd.com/mental-health/what-are-symptoms-ptsd
https://samehereglobal.org/ptsd-prof
ile/?gclid=CjwKCAjwxev3BRBBEiwAiB_

Made in the USA
Coppell, TX
21 December 2020

46901629R00105